D1305061

DIRTY FOOD

DIRTY FOOD

Over 65 devilishly delicious recipes
for the best worst food you'll ever eat!

Carol Hilker

photography by
Peter Cassidy

rps
LONDON • NEW YORK

Dirty Food is dedicated to my friends. My mad, crazy, hungry, food snob, gluttonous friends.

Senior Designer Iona Hoyle

Commissioning Editor Nathan Joyce

Production Gary Hayes

Editorial Director Julia Charles

Art Director Leslie Harrington

Prop Stylist Tony Hutchinson

Food Stylists Lizzie Harris & Emily Kydd

Indexer Hilary Bird

First published in the UK in 2014

by Ryland Peters & Small

20–21 Jockey's Fields

London WC1R 4BW

and

519 Broadway, 5th Floor

New York, NY 10012

www.rylandpeters.com

10 9 8 7 6 5 4 3 2 1

Text © Carol Hilker 2014

Design and photographs
© Ryland Peters & Small 2014

ISBN: 978-1-84975-491-0

A CIP record for this book is available from the British Library

A CIP record for this book is available from the Library of Congress

Printed in China

Notes

• All spoon measurements are level unless otherwise specified.

• Ovens should be preheated to the specified temperature. Recipes in this book were tested using a regular oven. If using a fan-assisted oven, follow the manufacturer's instructions for adjusting temperatures.

• Eggs used in this book are (UK) medium and (US) large unless otherwise stated

CONTENTS

INTRODUCTION

This book is a guilty pleasure. A lust letter (or perhaps a dirty text) to food, cherry-picking the most wild, delicious and fun dishes we could think of, in most cases reinventing some of the most beloved comfort food. There will always be an almost primal desire to go back to what we knew and loved as a kid, and food was a big part of that. However, as the world moves forward at rampant speed, the same old baked chicken or mac 'n' cheese recipe just won't cut it anymore. We crave more complex textures and bolder flavours.

This book is the answer. Grown-up comfort food. Decadent, delicious....and dirty.

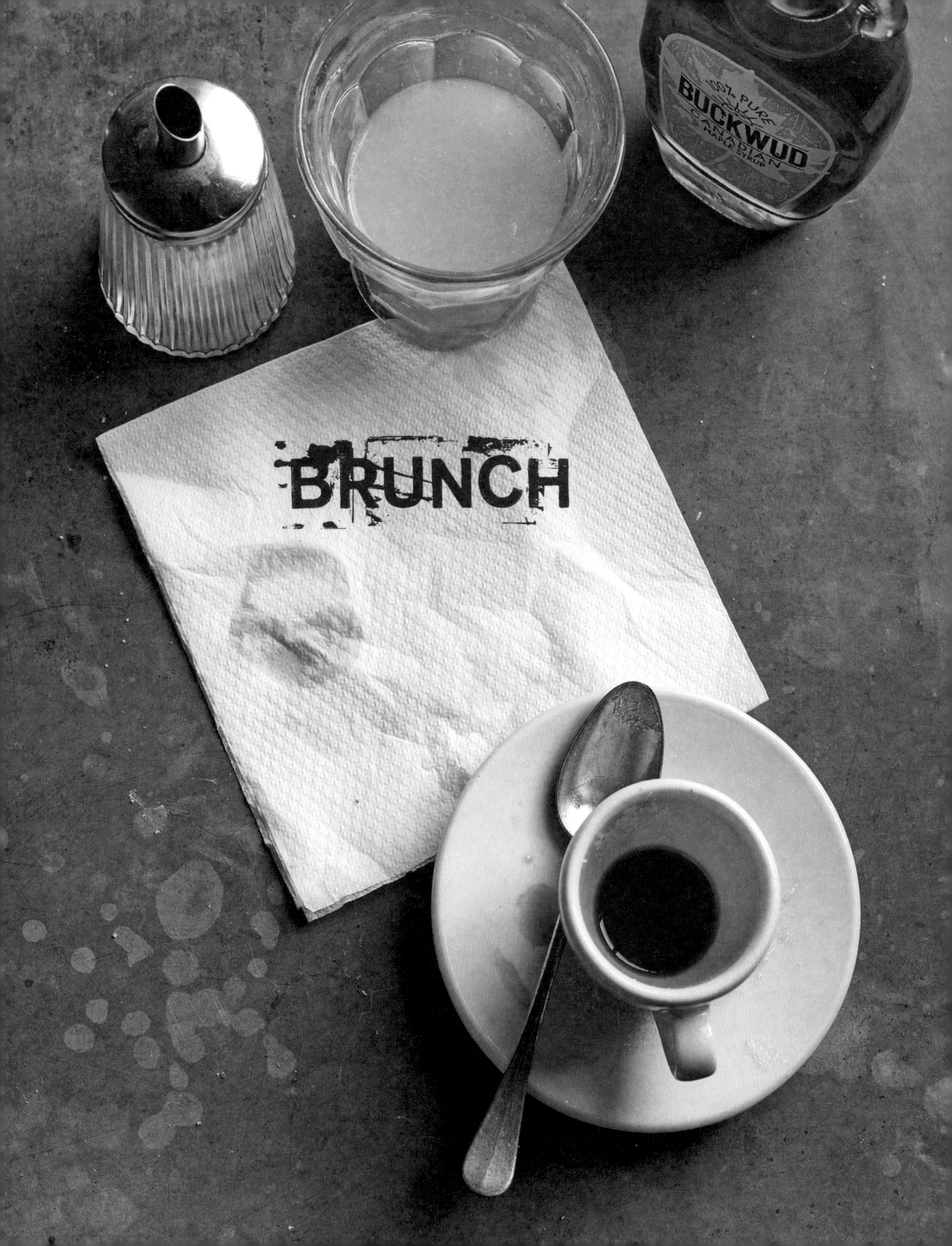
100% PURE
BUCKWUD
CANADIAN
MAPLE SYRUP
BRUNCH

The pretzel croissant is a wonderful twist on a traditional French pastry.
It does need to be prepared the day before you want to bake and eat it,
but it is seriously worth the effort!

pretzel croissant

500 ml/2 cups cold milk

2 tablespoons honey

600 g/4½ cups bread flour,
plus more for dusting

65 g/½ cup pastry flour

100 g/½ cup granulated
sugar

40 g/1½ oz. fresh yeast,
crumbled

1 tablespoon plus 1½
teaspoons sea salt

575 g/5 sticks unsalted
butter, very cold

1 large egg, lightly beaten

enough sea salt and white
sesame seeds to sprinkle over
the dough

**electric mixer fitted with
a dough hook**

pizza cutter

makes 12–16

Pour the milk and honey into a large measuring cup or jug/pitcher. Stir to combine.

Fit an electric mixer with a dough hook and incorporate the bread flour, pastry flour, sugar, yeast and salt. Stir to combine. Add the milk and honey and mix on low speed until the dough is just coming together, about 2½ minutes.

Turn out the dough onto a lightly floured cutting board or work surface and knead for about 45 seconds, forming a smooth ball. Wrap in clingfilm/plastic wrap and place in the refrigerator for about 1 hour.

Meanwhile, unwrap the butter and lay out the sticks side by side on clingfilm/plastic wrap. Sprinkle the butter with bread flour. Pound the butter and flour with a rolling pin until the flour is incorporated into the butter. Roll into a 20 cm/8-in square. Wrap tightly in clingfilm/plastic wrap and refrigerate for 1 hour.

Remove the dough ball from the refrigerator, unwrap and place on a lightly floured surface. Roll into a 40 x 25-cm/16 x 10-in. rectangle with a thickness of 1.25 cm/ ½ in. The short side should face you. Brush off excess flour. Remove the butter from the refrigerator and place it on top of the dough.

Starting at the farthest side from you, fold the top half of the rectangle over the butter. Repeat with the side closest to you, overlapping. Flip the dough and butter mixture over, facing the seams down. Roll the dough until the butter and dough come together.

Next, roll the croissant dough out into another 40 x 25-cm/16 x 10-in. rectangle. Fold the bottom third of the rectangle over, then fold the top third over. You now have 3 rectangular pieces of dough piled on top of each other. Wrap the dough in clingfilm/plastic wrap and put in the refrigerator for 1 hour.

Repeat the rolling and folding process (detailed in the last paragraph) twice, remembering to refrigerate the dough again for an hour. After the final time, refrigerate the dough one more time, 6–8 hours to overnight.

Turn the dough onto a lightly floured cutting board or work surface. Roll the dough into a 76 x 40-cm/30 x 16-in. rectangle. Use a pizza cutter to cut the dough into triangles; each should have a 10 cm/4 in. bottom. Cut a slit into the centre of the base of each triangle. Place the triangles side by side on a clean work surface.

Form each triangle into a croissant; to shape them, stretch the lower half of the triangle, expanding the slit. Fold the inner corners formed by the slit towards the outer sides of the triangle, pressing down to seal the croissant.

Using your fingertips, roll the base of the triangle away from you, upward. Stretch the dough slightly outward as you roll. The tip should be tucked under. Place the two ends toward you to form a crescent. Transfer to a baking sheet, with the dough pieces 5 cm/2 in. apart. Cover with clingfilm/plastic wrap and let rise in a warm spot for 1 hour. They should have doubled in size and should now be very spongy.

Preheat an oven to 200°C (400°F) Gas 6. Brush the croissants with the beaten egg wash and sprinkle with sea salt and sesame seeds. Bake for 20–25 minutes, rotating half-way through until the croissants are puffed and golden. Cool on a wire rack before serving.

According to food lore, the omelette has been around since the 16th century. Since then, many variations have emerged, from the ham, green (bell) pepper and onion combination in a Denver omelette to khagineh, an Iranian version in which eggs are beaten with sugar. The lobster omelette is popular on the East coast of the US, and is especially decadent when served with truffle-hollandaise sauce.

Maine lobster omelette

for the truffle-Hollandaise sauce

3 egg yolks

60 ml/¼ cup water

2 tablespoons freshly squeezed lemon juice

115 g/1 stick cold, unsalted butter cut into pieces

¼ teaspoon sea salt

pinch of ground black pepper

pinch of paprika

drizzle of truffle oil

1 chive, chopped, to garnish

for the omelette

6 eggs

170 g/6 oz. fresh lobster meat, chopped

2 teaspoons unsalted butter

sea salt and ground black pepper

115 g/4 oz. tomatoes, chopped

1 teaspoon chives, chopped

serves 2

Preheat an oven to 100°C (210°F).

To make the truffle-Hollandaise sauce, whisk the egg yolks, water and lemon juice in a small saucepan until blended. Cook over a very low heat, stirring constantly, until the mixture bubbles at the edges. Stir in the butter, a piece at a time, until it has melted and until the sauce has thickened. Remove from the heat immediately and stir in the salt, pepper, paprika and truffle oil. Transfer the sauce to a small pot, ready to serve.

Whisk the eggs together, then separate the mixture into two bowls and set aside.

Spread the lobster onto an oven-proof dish and place in the preheated oven for 5 minutes.

Over a medium heat, warm a medium to large non-stick frying pan/skillet and add 1 teaspoon of the butter. As the butter melts, season one portion of the eggs with salt and black pepper. Add this egg mixture to the heated frying pan/skillet and stir gently with a spatula.

As the eggs start to set, add half the chopped lobster, half the tomatoes and half the chives to the eggs and stir gently. As the eggs start to set, stop stirring and allow them to form for 1–2 minutes. Fold the omelette and slide it out onto a warm plate. Place the plate in the oven to keep the omelette warm. Repeat the same process for the second omelette.

This variant on a traditional French breakfast comes with bacon, brie and poached eggs, all assembled on top of a pretzel croissant and drizzled with Hollandaise sauce. This decadent and delicious dish makes the pefect lazy Sunday brunch or, if you're in the mood, a fun breakfast-for-dinner.

Paris-style eggs Benedict

for the hollandaise sauce

140 g/1¼ sticks unsalted butter

3 egg yolks

1 tablespoon lemon juice

½ teaspoon salt

for the eggs Benedict

60 g/½ stick butter

4 slices bacon

2 teaspoons white or rice vinegar

8 slices Brie cheese

4 eggs

4 Pretzel Croissants (page 10)

butter, for spreading

dash of Tabasco sauce (optional)

couple of sprigs flat-leaf parsley, chopped, to garnish

ground black pepper, to taste

serves 4

To make the Hollandaise sauce, melt the butter in a small saucepan. Put the egg yolks, lemon juice and salt in a blender and blend on medium to medium-high speed for 25 seconds or until the eggs lighten in colour. Change the blender speed to the lowest setting and very slowly, pour in the hot butter and continue to blend. Add salt and lemon juice to taste. Transfer to a small jug/pitcher.

Melt some butter in a large frying pan/skillet on a low to medium heat, and when the pan is hot, add the bacon, turning it occasionally until warm.

While the bacon is cooking, fill a large saucepan with water and bring to the boil. Add the vinegar and let it come to a boil again. After the water boils, reduce the heat to a simmer.

Next, poach the eggs. The easiest way is to do one egg at a time. Crack the egg into a small bowl and slip it into the barely simmering water. Once the egg begins to solidify, slip in the next egg and so on until you have all 4 cooking. Turn the heat off, cover the pan with a lid and let the eggs sit for 3–4 minutes, depending on how runny you like your eggs. Starting with the first egg you cracked, gently lift them out with a slotted spoon and set them down in a bowl or on a plate.

Toast and butter the croissants. Top with the bacon, 2 slices of Brie and a poached egg. Sprinkle on Tabasco sauce if desired. Pour the Hollandaise sauce over the top and garnish with flat-leaf parsley and ground black pepper to taste.

This brunch skillet is a new take on the traditional steak and eggs combination. Don't be afraid to substitute some of the vegetables for more seasonal selections. Fry, scramble or poach the eggs – there are many ways to give this brunch favourite your own twist!

steak & egg brunch skillet

3 tablespoons olive oil

1 onion, chopped

2 carrots, chopped

3 sticks celery, chopped

1 clove garlic, halved

3 tablespoons tomato purée/paste

250 ml/1 cup red wine

2 litres/1³/₄ quarts chicken stock

4 tablespoons packed brown sugar

80 ml/¹/₃ cup Worcestershire sauce

2 tablespoons soy sauce

1 handful fresh thyme

3 fresh bay leaves

sea salt and ground black pepper

4–5 beef thin/short rib(s), boneless, uncooked

for the hash

120 g/¹/₂ cup potatoes, diced

butter, for frying

1 tablespoon olive oil

¹/₂ onion, diced

1 shallot, minced

2 cloves garlic, minced

a few sprigs fresh thyme, to serve

a few sprigs flat-leaf parsley, chopped, to serve

sea salt and ground black pepper, to taste

1 fried egg, to serve

Hollandaise sauce (page 14), to serve

serves 4

Preheat the oven to 150°C (300°F) Gas 2.

Add the olive oil to an oven-safe frying pan/skillet and over a medium heat caramelize the onion, carrots, celery and garlic. Add the tomato purée/paste and cook for 1–2 minutes. Add the red wine and reduce the mixture by half. Add the stock, brown sugar, Worcestershire sauce, soy sauce, thyme and bay leaves. Season generously with salt and pepper and boil. Add the thin/short rib(s) and transfer the pan to the preheated oven for 2 hours or until the meat is tender. Remove the pan from the oven, strain and reserve the liquid and discard the vegetables and herbs. Over a medium heat, boil the reserved liquid to skim off the fat and reduce the liquid until it coats the back of a spoon. Set this braising liquid aside while you make the hash.

For the hash, fill a saucepan with water and bring to a boil. Blanch the potatoes until they are tender. Drain them and run them under cold water to stop from cooking. Heat up a frying pan/skillet with the butter, add the potatoes and fry until lightly brown. Set aside. Add the olive oil to the frying pan/skillet and over a medium heat, caramelize the onion. Add the shallot and garlic and continue cooking until the mixture is golden.

Dice the thin/short rib(s), and add the potatoes, onion, shallot and garlic. Add the reserved braising liquid to moisten and mix in the thyme, flat-leaf parsley and potatoes. Season to taste with salt and pepper. Serve with a fried egg on top and with Hollandaise sauce on the side.

French toast in itself is a decadent breakfast, but adding banana bread really jazzes up this morning treat. Feel free to use caramel sauce instead of maple syrup.

banana bread french toast

for the banana bread

280 g/2 cups plain/all-purpose flour

1 teaspoon baking powder

1/4 teaspoon salt

115 g/1 stick butter

150 g/3/4 cup brown sugar

2 eggs, beaten

5 ripe, mashed bananas

for the French toast

3 eggs

3 tablespoons sweetened condensed milk

1 teaspoon vanilla extract or paste

2 tablespoons butter

1 loaf banana bread (see above)

icing/confectioners' sugar for dusting

maple syrup

1 loaf pan (23 x 13 cm/9 x 5 in.), lightly greased

serves 4

Preheat an oven to 180°C (350°F) Gas 4. Prepare the loaf pan.

In a large bowl, combine the flour, baking powder and salt. In a separate medium bowl, cream together the butter and brown sugar. Stir the eggs in one at a time and add the mashed bananas until combined. Add the banana mixture to the flour mixture and stir with a wooden spoon until mixed together. Pour into the greased loaf pan. Bake for 1 hour, or until a cocktail stick/toothpick inserted into the centre comes out clean. Let cool for 5–10 minutes and then turn it out onto a wire rack.

In a small-medium bowl, beat the eggs, sweetened condensed milk and vanilla with a fork. Set aside.

Melt the butter in a large frying pan/skillet over a medium heat. Slice the banana bread into 4 thick slices. Dip each slice into the egg mixture and place into the hot frying pan/skillet. Cook on each side for 1–2 minutes until golden brown. Plate and dust with icing/confectioners' sugar. Serve with a side of maple syrup.

Blueberry cotton candy pancakes mix a little bit of fairground nostalgia into breakfast, so this dish is perfect for a dreary Monday morning. The tartness of the blueberries balance out the sweet flavour of the cotton candy flavouring to make a fun breakfast, dessert or snack.

blueberry cotton candy pancakes

for the pancakes

200 g/1½ cups plain/all-purpose flour

1 tablespoon granulated white sugar

1 tablespoon brown sugar

1 teaspoon baking powder

½ teaspoon bicarbonate of/ baking soda

½ teaspoon salt

2 eggs, at room temperature

250 ml/1 cup milk

235 g/1 cup sour cream or plain Greek yogurt

115 g/1 stick butter, melted

6 drops cotton candy flavouring

½ teaspoon vanilla extract

225 g/1½ cups fresh or frozen blueberries, plus extra to serve

maple syrup, to serve

for the maple whipped cream

1½ tablespoons maple syrup

500 ml/2 cups single/light cream

serves 4

[handwritten notes: in big meas. cup; in 4C; 4T; add →; use ⅓ C measure to make pancakes]

Sift or whisk the dry ingredients (flour, sugars, baking powder, bicarbonate of/baking soda and salt) together in a large mixing bowl. In a separate large bowl, lightly whisk the eggs. Add the milk and the sour cream or Greek yogurt, half the melted butter, the cotton candy flavouring and the vanilla, whisking to incorporate.

Make a well in the dry ingredients and pour the egg mixture into it. Whisk the ingredients together until combined, then fold the blueberries into the batter.

Heat a large frying pan/skillet over a medium heat and coat with some of the remaining melted butter. Pour a small ladleful of the batter into the centre of the pan. When bubbles begin to form and "pop" on the pancake's surface, after about 1 minute, and the outer edge looks done, flip it over and cook briefly for about 30 seconds on the other side. Transfer to a warm plate until ready to serve. Repeat until the batter is used up, adding a little butter to the pan each time before adding the batter.

To make the maple whipped cream, add the cream and the maple syrup to a mixing bowl and whisk with a hand-mixer or a free standing-mixer until the whipped cream forms soft peaks.

Serve with extra maple syrup and fresh blueberries.

This recipe takes the delightfully salty and sweet flavour of maple-cured bacon, along with vanilla and cinnamon, to really liven up the everyday waffle.

Belgian waffle with maple-cured bacon

3 eggs, separated

360 ml/1½ cups buttermilk

115 g/1 stick unsalted butter, melted and cooled

½ teaspoon vanilla paste, extract or ½ a vanilla pod/bean

200 g/1½ cups plain/all-purpose flour

1 teaspoon bicarbonate of/baking soda

1½ teaspoons baking powder

¼ teaspoon salt

3 tablespoons granulated sugar

½ teaspoon ground cinnamon

pre-bought thin cut maple-cured bacon (or follow the recipe on page 35 to make your own), 1 slice per waffle

softened butter or ice cream, to serve

maple syrup, to serve

waffle maker

serves 4

Note: Measure out all the ingredients ahead of time. This will help the recipe come together quickly. You also want to make sure that you have all the ingredients at room temperature.

Preheat an oven to 110°C (225°F) Gas ¼ and turn on the waffle maker following the manufacturer's instructions.

In a large bowl, whisk the egg yolks. Slowly incorporate the buttermilk, butter and vanilla. In a separate medium bowl, sift together the flour, bicarbonate of/baking soda, baking powder, salt, sugar and cinnamon. Add the flour mixture to the egg mixture and whisk until smooth.

In another medium bowl, using a hand or free-standing mixer, whisk the egg whites until they form stiff peaks. Using a rubber spatula, fold half of the egg whites into the batter and incorporate well. After they're incorporated, fold in the remaining egg whites.

Put enough batter into the waffle maker to make a waffle and place one piece of raw bacon on top of the batter. Cook the waffle according to the manufacturer's instructions, then transfer it to a baking sheet and place it in the preheated oven to keep warm. Repeat the process again to make each waffle.

Serve the waffles with softened butter or ice cream and some really good maple syrup.

I think it's time that quinoa jumped off the healthy lunch plate and into something a little sexier. So I've led it astray with maple syrup, brown sugar, vanilla and cinnamon. Who says that gluten-free can't dabble with decadence? Feel free to add bananas, raisins, berries or honey just before taking the pan off the heat.

quinoa porridge with maple syrup & brown sugar

500 ml/2 cups milk, almond milk, rice milk, light coconut milk or vanilla almond milk

170 g/1 cup quinoa

1/4 teaspoon salt

3 tablespoons packed brown sugar

2 tablespoons maple syrup

1/4 teaspoon cinnamon

1 teaspoon vanilla extract

chopped nuts and fruit, to serve (optional)

serves 2–4

In a medium saucepan, pour in the milk and heat over a medium heat. Stir constantly with a wooden spatula, wooden spoon, or whisk. Gently scrape the bottom of the pan periodically until the milk begins to bubble and simmer, about 5–10 minutes.

When the milk simmers, add the quinoa and salt and stir until combined. Let the quinoa come to a slow boil. Cover the pan, leaving the lid slightly ajar to vent and reduce the heat to low. Let the mixture cook on a low simmer for 10 minutes. After this time, remove the lid and stir in the brown sugar, maple syrup and cinnamon.

Place the lid loosely back on the saucepan and let the quinoa simmer on low for about 10 more minutes. Check and stir occasionally until most of the liquid is absorbed and the quinoa is tender. Reduce the heat if the quinoa appears to be simmering too quickly; add additional milk if it becomes too dry before it's tender. When done, the quinoa should look like a cross between porridge and cream of wheat. At this point, remove from heat, add the vanilla and stir. Dish into 2 big bowls or 4 little bowls and add chopped nuts and fruit if desired.

BURGERS

RIBS & FRIES

HOT & COLD
SANDWICHES

This French bread is crispy on the outside and soft on the inside. It's perfect for almost any sandwich recipe and makes a wonderful addition to a dinner as table bread. Even stale French country bread is useful, as it makes fantastic croutons. There are so many uses for this bread that it will quickly become part of your repertoire.

French country bread

500 ml/2 cups water, heated to 43°C/110°F

1 teaspoon granulated sugar

3¼ teaspoons active dry yeast

700–775 g/5–5½ cups strong white bread flour (plus additional flour for dusting)

2½ teaspoons salt

non-stick cooking spray

1 egg white, lightly beaten with a pinch of salt

kitchen thermometer

electric mixer fitted with a dough hook

makes 2 loaves

In a small bowl, combine the warm water and sugar, stirring until the sugar dissolves. Add the yeast and stir gently to mix. Let stand until foamy, about 5 minutes.

In the bowl of an electric mixer fitted with a dough hook, combine 550 g/4 cups of the flour and the salt. Beat on low speed until combined. Slowly add the yeast mixture and beat for about 1 minute until incorporated. Increase the speed to medium-low to medium and beat for 10 minutes adding more flour, about 30 g/¼ cup at a time, until the dough is elastic and pulls away from the sides of the bowl.

Turn the dough out onto a lightly floured surface and knead for 1 minute. Form into a ball and dust lightly with flour. Sprinkle a little flour into a large bowl and transfer the dough to the bowl. Cover with clingfilm/plastic wrap and let the dough rise in a warm place until it has doubled in bulk, around 45–60 minutes.

Turn the dough out back onto the lightly floured surface. Punch down the dough (to remove any air pockets) and knead for a few seconds. Form the dough into a ball and return to the bowl again. Cover the bowl with clingfilm/plastic wrap and let the dough rise again in a warm place until doubled in bulk, around 20–30 minutes.

Turn the dough onto the lightly floured surface and punch down again. Cut the dough into 2 equal pieces and shape each into a ball. Let rest for 5 minutes.

Line a bread pan with a clean tea/dish towel and sprinkle with a little flour.

Roll each ball into a log with tapered ends, about the length of the pan, and place on the towel in the pan. Cover with the overhanging edges of the towel and let rise in a warm place for 20 minutes.

Position an oven rack in the lowest position of the oven, and place a baking pan a third-full of boiling water onto the rack. Preheat an oven to 220°C (425°F) Gas 7.

Gently lift the towels off, taking care not to let the loaves touch each other and set them down on a work surface. Spray the pan with non-stick cooking spray and, using the towel as a guide, gently flip each loaf into a well in the pan. Brush off excess flour.

Using a sharp knife, make 3–5 diagonal slashes in the loaves about 6mm/¼ in. deep. Brush with the beaten egg white mixture. Bake on the centre rack of the preheated oven until the bread is golden brown and sounds hollow when tapped, about 30–35 minutes. Transfer the loaves to a wire rack until they reach room temperature.

It's only been over the last 10 years that pretzels have deviated from their conventional twisted pattern to a bun-shape. This recipe is simple, uses just a handful of ingredients, and makes the perfect accompaniment to any sandwich or as a side with any lunch or dinner.

pretzel buns

350 ml/1½ cups water, warmed to 40–50°C (105–115°F)

1 x 7g/¼ oz. sachet fast-action dried yeast

2–3 tablespoons olive oil or canola oil, for coating

600 g/4½ cups plain/all-purpose flour, plus more for dusting the work surface

2 teaspoons sea salt, plus extra for sprinkling

1 tablespoon granulated sugar

4 tablespoons unsalted butter, melted

vegetable oil

55 g/¼ cup bicarbonate of/ baking soda

1 egg, lightly beaten

kitchen thermometer

electric mixer fitted with a dough hook

baking sheet lined with parchment paper, oiled

makes 6–8

Tip the warmed water into the bowl of a free-standing mixer (or a mixing bowl if you don't have a free-standing mixer). Sprinkle the yeast on top and set aside until the mixture bubbles a little, about 5 minutes.

Mix together the flour, salt and sugar, then add to the yeast mixture, along with the melted butter. Using the dough hook attachment, mix on the lowest setting until everything comes together. Increase the speed and continue mixing until the dough becomes elastic and smooth, about 8–10 minutes. If you don't have a free-standing mixer, combine the ingredients using a wooden spoon, then knead by hand on a lightly floured work surface for 10–15 minutes. Form the dough into a ball and place in a lightly oiled bowl, cover with oiled clingfilm/plastic wrap and leave to rise until doubled in size, about 1 hour.

Prepare the baking sheet. Punch down the risen dough and knead briefly on a lightly floured work surface. Divide the dough into 8 equal pieces and shape into round rolls. Place the rolls on the oiled parchment paper, cover with oiled clingfilm/plastic wrap and leave to rise until almost doubled in size, about 30 minutes.

Preheat an oven to 220°C (425°F) Gas 7. Fill a large saucepan with water, so that it reaches one-third of the way up the sides, and bring to the boil. Remove from the heat and add the baking soda, then return to a simmer. Gently lower 2–3 of the buns into the simmering water and poach for 30 seconds on each side. Remove using a slotted spoon and return to the parchment paper, seam side down. Repeat with the remaining buns.

Brush the buns all over with the beaten egg and sprinkle with a little salt. Using a sharp knife cut a cross in the top of each one. Bake for 20–30 minutes in the preheated oven until golden brown.

Pulled pork pretzel buns are the best thing to make with a pork shoulder. It takes very little work to create an easy and delicious slow-cooked sandwich filling with or without sauce. The secret to this pulled pork is the addition of India pale ale (IPA) and apple cider vinegar to make the sauce.

pulled pork pretzel buns

2 medium yellow onions, thinly sliced

4 medium garlic cloves, thinly sliced

120 ml/½ cup apple cider vinegar

120 ml/½ cup India pale ale

1 fresh sage leaf

1 tablespoon packed dark brown sugar

1 tablespoon chilli powder

1 tablespoon sea salt, plus more as needed

1 teaspoon ground black pepper

½ teaspoon ground cumin

¼ teaspoon ground cinnamon

1 (2¼ kg/5 lbs.) boneless or bone-in pork shoulder, twine or netting removed

450 g/2 cups BBQ Sauce (page 64), optional

6 Pretzel Buns (page 31)

butter, for spreading

Rosemary Coleslaw (page 110), to serve

slow cooker

serves 6

Place the onions and garlic in an even layer in the slow cooker, pour in the vinegar, beer and add the sage leaf.

Combine the sugar, chilli powder, salt, pepper, cumin and cinnamon in a small bowl. Pat the pork dry with paper towels. Rub the spice mixture all over the pork and place the meat on top of the onions and garlic. Cover and cook until the pork is fork tender, about 6–8 hours on a high setting or 8–10 hours on low.

Meanwhile, follow the instructions on page 31 to make the pretzel buns.

Turn off the slow cooker and move the pork to a cutting board. Set a fine-mesh sieve/strainer over a medium heat-proof bowl. Pour the onion mixture from the slow cooker through the sieve/strainer and return the solids to the slow cooker. Set the strained liquid aside and use a spoon to skim and discard any fat from the surface.

If the pork has a bone, remove and discard it. Using 2 forks, shred the pork, discarding any large pieces of fat. Return the shredded meat to the slow cooker and add the BBQ sauce, if using, and mix to combine. Add 60 ml/¼ cup of the strained liquid at a time to the slow cooker until the pork is just moistened. Taste and season with salt as needed.

Cut each pretzel bun in half and butter the bottom. Lay a generous helping of pork onto each bun, spoon over the sauce and top with rosemary coleslaw. Serve with yellow mustard and a refreshing glass of Homemade Lemonade (page 153).

There's no turning back once you've tried homemade maple-cured bacon, although you will need to prepare it a week in advance. When it's ready, just try to stop yourself frying up the whole lot and working your way through it with sticky fingers and guilty pleasure.

maple-cured bacon & tomato sandwich

for the maple-cured bacon

140 g/1 cup sea salt

400 g/2 cups brown sugar (preferably dark brown sugar)

320 g/1 cup pure maple syrup

2.25–4.5 kg/5–10 lbs. pork belly, washed and patted dry, with the skin left on

for the sandwich

8 slices sourdough bread

2 tablespoons mayonnaise

4 eggs, cooked on both sides (optional)

8 tomato slices

4 slices Cheddar cheese (optional)

maple cured bacon (see above), 2 slices per sandwich

handful of rocket/arugula

sea salt and ground black pepper

Sweet Pickles (page 125)

Sweet Potato Fries (page 114)

serves 4

Curing bacon at home takes a while, but it's really worth it. In a medium bowl, combine the salt, sugar and maple syrup. Rub the mixture over the pork belly on both sides. Place the pork in a large resealable plastic bag with a zip and seal tightly. Refrigerate and let cure for 7 days, turning once a day.

After 7 days, the bacon will be cured. Cut off a small piece and fry it to test the saltiness of the bacon. If the bacon doesn't taste too salty after being cooked, you are ready to proceed. If the bacon tastes too salty, soak the remaining pork belly in cold water for 1 hour.

Once the bacon is ready to cook, carefully slice it into strips of the desired thickness. Fry it for 3–4 minutes per side, until it reaches the crispiness that you like. Fry the eggs, if using.

Assemble the sandwiches with slices of sourdough bread, mayonnaise, eggs (if using), tomatoes, Cheddar cheese (if using), rocket/arugula, salt and pepper. Serve with sweet pickles and sweet potato fries.

Chicago-style hot dogs are the epitome of comfort food for anyone who has grown up in or near the Windy City. This recipe will take a day or two to prepare, as it involves making the hot dogs themselves, but it will be worth the wait!

homemade Chicago-style hot dog on a pretzel croissant

900 g/2 lbs. all-beef chuck

675 g/1 1/2 lbs. boneless thin/short rib

1 teaspoon sea salt

1 teaspoon pink curing salt

250 ml/1 cup iced water

1 tablespoon dry mustard

2 teaspoons paprika

1 teaspoon ground coriander

1/4 teaspoon ground black pepper

1 tablespoon garlic, minced

2 tablespoons light corn syrup

16–20 Pretzel Croissants (page 10)

yellow mustard, to serve

Spicy Dill Pickles (page 125), to serve

1 medium tomato, sliced, to serve

handful of jalapeño or sport peppers, to serve

1 onion, diced, to serve

celery salt to taste, to serve

Hand-cut Fries (page 113), to serve

meat grinder

sausage stuffer and 16—20 sausage casings

makes **16–20**

Chop the thin/short ribs into small squares and then run the beef chuck and thin/short rib through a meat grinder on a medium setting. Add the salt, pink salt and iced water to the meat mixture. Incorporate together with your hands and place in a large bowl, covered with clingfilm/plastic wrap. Let the meat mixture sit in the refrigerator for 1–2 days.

In a mixing bowl, mix the mustard, paprika, ground coriander, ground black pepper and garlic.

Remove the meat from the refrigerator and add the mustard mix, along with the corn syrup. Mix together with your hands until everything is evenly distributed.

Spread the mixture evenly on a baking sheet and place in the freezer for 45 minutes.

Remove the meat from the freezer and put it through the meat grinder again, on the smallest grind setting possible. Then measure out the meat in thirds and place each third separately in a food processor, processing until the meat has the consistency of paste. Don't process all the meat at once, as it will be harder to evenly process.

Fit a sausage stuffer with the sausage casings, stuff with the meat paste and seal according to the manufacturer's instructions. If you don't have a sausage stuffer, you can also hand stuff the hot dogs into the casings.

Put the hot dogs in the refrigerator until ready to cook.

Preheat an oven to 180°C (350°F) Gas 4.

Place the hot dogs on a baking sheet and cook for 20 minutes, turning once half-way through cooking. They can also be grilled or boiled.

Lightly butter and place the croissants in the oven briefly to toast. Take out, cut lengthwise almost all the way through and put the hog dog into the croissant. Add the toppings and serve with hand-cut fries.

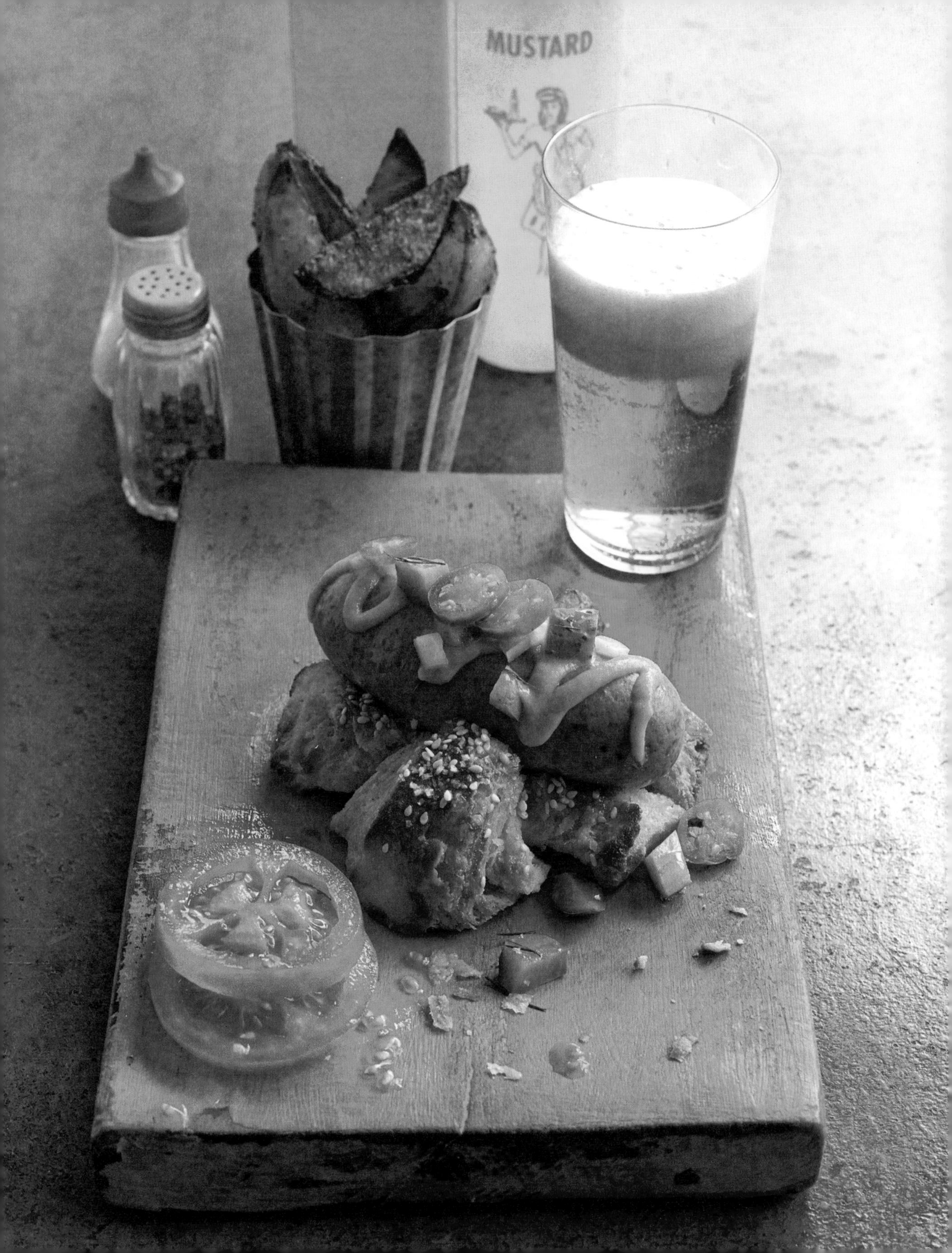
MUSTARD

The club sandwich made its debut in **1899**. It is thought that the birthplace of this famous sandwich, also known as the "clubhouse sandwich", is in Saratoga Springs, New York, a legendary horse-racing town. This version pairs sourdough bread with Dijonnaise, cured tomatoes, maple-cured bacon and cured ham to elevate this sandwich to the next level.

club sandwich

12 slices sourdough bread

2 medium avocados

8 cos/romaine lettuce leaves

175 g/^{3}/$_4$ cup mayonnaise or Dijonnaise (page 43)

3 large tomatoes, cut into 16 thick slices

16 slices Maple-Cured Bacon (page 35) or regular bacon

8 slices roasted turkey breast

16 slices cured ham

8 slices Fontina cheese

sea salt and ground black pepper to taste

16 cocktail sticks/toothpicks

makes 4

Toast the sourdough bread under a grill/broiler on both sides. Pit/stone, peel and slice the avocados. Finely chop the lettuce and arrange it into 8 stacks.

Arrange 3 bread slices in a row. Spread 1 tablespoon of Dijonnaise over 1 side of each slice of bread. Place a lettuce stack on the top of the first slice of bread. Top with 2 tomato slices, a few slices of avocado and season with salt and pepper if needed. Place 2 slices of bacon on top, then a slice of turkey, 2 slices of ham and a slice of the Fontina cheese. Season with salt and pepper. Place the second bread slice on top and repeat the layering. Cover with the third bread slice, Dijonnaise side down.

Pin the sandwich together by piercing it with 4 cocktail sticks/toothpicks arranged in a diamond pattern. Repeat the whole process again to form another 3 sandwiches.

A good steak sandwich isn't always the easiest to come by. It's hard to find the right combination of perfectly spiced steak, topped with a bounty of trimmings that add the right amount of flavour and texture when placed on a crispy loaf of bread. This sandwich, with rare steak, sautéed onions, Dijonnaise, rocket/arugula and blue cheese on French country bread is the answer!

steak sandwich with sautéed onions & blue cheese

2 x 350 g/12 oz. sirloin /New York strip steaks, cut 2.5 cm/1 in. thick

olive oil, for frying

4 onions, sliced into rings

½ teaspoon fresh thyme leaves

2 garlic cloves, minced

1–2 loaves French Country Bread (page 30)

4 tablespoons Dijonnaise (page 43)

30 g/1 cup rocket/arugula

115–225 g/4–8 oz. blue cheese, crumbled

sea salt and ground black pepper

Hand-cut Fries (page 113), to serve

makes 4

Season the steaks with salt and pepper on both sides. Heat 2–4 tablespoons of olive oil in a medium frying pan/skillet over a high heat until it's very hot, almost smoking. Sear the steaks for 1½ minutes per side and then reduce the heat to low and cook the steaks for about 3–4 minutes, turning once. Remove the steaks from the pan and place on a plate. Cover tightly with foil and allow to sit in the refrigerator for 10 minutes. Remove and slice the steak into strips.

Using the same frying pan/skillet, heat 3 tablespoons more olive oil over a medium heat. Add the onion slices and thyme and sauté for 10 minutes, stirring occasionally, until the onion is caramelized. Add the garlic for the last 1–2 minutes.

Cut the French country bread lengthwise and into large sandwich rolls. Spread 1 tablespoon Dijonnaise on the bottom half of each bun. Place a layer of the steak strips on top of the Dijonnaise, sprinkle with salt and pepper and top with the caramelized onion rings. Place the rocket/arugula on top of the onion rings and sprinkle a handful of blue cheese on top. Cover with the top half of the buns.

Serve with hand-cut fries.

According to food historians, the cheeseburger was invented in 1920 in Pasadena, California, a remarkable 20 years after the hamburger first appeared. Lionel Sternberger (no pun intended), a cook at his father's sandwich shop, "The Rite Spot", one day decided to place a slab of American cheese on a hamburger, inventing one of the world's most loved sandwiches.

diner cheeseburger

for the Dijonnaise

2 large white onions

2 tablespoons butter

400 ml/1¾ cups single/light cream

3 tablespoons Dijon mustard

pinch of salt, ground black pepper, garlic, nutmeg, chopped fresh flat-leaf parsley and tarragon

for the cheeseburgers

450 g/1 lb. minced/ground beef

140 g/1 cup onion, minced

2 garlic cloves, pressed

8 slices Maple-cured Bacon (page 35) or regular bacon

sea salt and ground black pepper

4 eggs

4 brioche buns

4 slices American or Cheddar cheese

1 Spicy Dill Pickle, chopped (page 125)

Sweet and Sour Pickle Relish (page 47), to serve

Hand-cut Fries (page 113), to serve

Ranch Dressing (page 56), to serve

makes 4

First, make the Dijonnaise by finely chopping the white onions and frying with the butter in a medium saucepan. Add the cream and mix in the mustard. Season the mixture and simmer until the sauce takes a mustardy colour and is relatively thick.

Mix together the minced/ground beef, minced onion and pressed garlic. Shape into patties and sprinkle with salt and pepper. Grill to your liking.

In a medium frying pan/skillet, fry 8 slices of maple-cured or regular bacon and 4 eggs, and set aside.

Cut a brioche bun in half and spread a layer of Dijonnaise. Place a cooked patty on top, then a slice of cheese, followed by a fried egg, 2 slices of bacon and some chopped dill pickle.

Serve with hand-cut fries, ranch dressing and sweet and sour pickle relish.

This sandwich takes the best of breakfast and dresses it up for lunch. The end result is a taste that melds salt beef, oozing Swiss cheese, egg and the simple seasoning of salt and pepper all on a toasted pretzel bun. It's the perfect egg sandwich. This recipe will involve a bit of preparation time, as it involves baking the pretzel buns in advance.

salt beef hash egg sandwich on a pretzel bun

4 Pretzel Buns (page 31)

60 g/½ stick unsalted butter

1 tablespoon olive oil

4 eggs

sea salt and ground black pepper

900 g/2 lbs. salt beef, thickly sliced

4–8 slices Swiss cheese

yellow mustard, to serve

4 gherkins/pickles, to serve

makes 4

Follow the recipe on page 31 to make 4 pretzel buns.

Heat the butter in a large frying pan/skillet on a medium-high heat. Add the olive oil and, after the butter starts to bubble, crack the eggs into the pan, being careful not to break the yolks. Season with salt and pepper. Fry the eggs to your liking and set aside.

Cut the pretzel buns in half and butter each side. Place a medium frying pan/skillet on the stove over a medium heat. Put the pretzel bun tops and bottoms butter side down in the pan/skillet for a few seconds until lightly toasted. Remove the buns, and add 2–3 slices of beef to the bun bottoms, followed by 1–2 slices of Swiss cheese and 1 fried egg. Place the pretzel bun top on top.

Serve immediately with yellow mustard and a pickle/gherkin.

Popularized in New York in the 1990s, this tasty mini-hamburger is in many ways the quintessential American burger.

sliders
with secret sauce

for the pickle relish

225 g/1 cup Sweet & Sour Pickles (page 125), finely chopped

1 small white onion, chopped

3 garlic cloves, minced

1 teaspoon sugar

1/4 teaspoon sea salt

for the sliders

450–680 g/1–1 1/2 lbs. extra lean minced/ground beef

2 spring onions/scallions, diced

1 teaspoon sea salt

1 teaspoon ground black pepper

1/2 tablespoon olive oil

1 egg

for the secret sauce

115 g/1/2 cup mayonnaise

2 tablespoons creamy French Dressing or Homemade Russian dressing (page 51)

3 tablespoons Pickle Relish (see above)

1/2 small white onion, finely diced

1 teaspoon vinegar

1 teaspoon granulated sugar

pinch of salt

to serve

8–12 slices American or Cheddar cheese

8–12 slider buns

iceberg lettuce, cut into strips

Spicy Dill Pickles (page 125), sliced

Sweet Potato Fries (page 114)

makes 8–12

Make the pickle relish in advance, by mixing all the ingredients in a bowl and storing in a jar or Tupperware container to marinade for at least 24 hours.

In a medium mixing bowl, combine the minced/ground beef, diced onions, salt, pepper, olive oil and egg. Mix well with your hands and then press the meat mixture into patties. You can use a cookie cutter to get even and equal-sized sliders. This recipe makes 8–12 sliders depending on the size you prefer.

In a small bowl, combine the secret sauce ingredients and season to taste.

Cook the sliders on a grill or pan-fry them to your liking. Place a slice of cheese on top of the hot slider to let it melt a little. Meanwhile, cut the slider buns in half and spread the secret sauce on the bottom half. Chop the iceberg lettuce into strips and and place a few on top of the sauce. Put the slider and cheese on top, followed by more secret sauce and a couple of sliced spicy dill pickles. Add the top half of the bun.

Serve the sliders warm with sweet potato fries and extra dill pickles.

There's probably no better comfort food than the grilled cheese sandwich. It is fantastically versatile, as it can be as simple or as pimped up as you like. This recipe is a major upgrade from the basic grilled cheese that I used to love as a kid!

ultimate grilled cheese sandwich

for the cured tomatoes

1–2 tomatoes

200 g/1 cup olive oil

60 g/1 cup homemade bread crumbs, toasted

pinch of salt

to assemble the sandwiches

12 slices thick-cut Maple-cured Bacon (page 35) or regular bacon

12 slices sourdough bread, cut 1.25 cm/$\frac{1}{2}$ in. thick

6 tablespoons salted butter, at room temperature

Dijonnaise (page 43)

25 g/$\frac{1}{4}$ cup Parmesan cheese, grated/shredded

115 g/4 oz. mature Cheddar cheese, grated/shredded

115 g/4 oz. Gouda cheese, grated/shredded

115 g/4 oz. Provolone cheese, grated/shredded

1$\frac{1}{2}$ teaspoons sea salt

$\frac{1}{2}$ teaspoon ground black pepper

oven-safe frying pan/skillet

makes 6

Slice the tomatoes to a thickness of 1.25 cm/$\frac{1}{2}$ in. Lay them in a pie dish and add olive oil until the slices are half-submerged. Let the tomatoes sit for 30 minutes, turning once. After that time, lift the tomatoes out of the oil and season them with salt. Press them into the homemade toasted bread crumbs.

Preheat an oven to 160°C (325°F) Gas 3.

Fry the bacon until nicely browned. Drain the slices on paper towels, let cool and cut into 2.5 cm/1-in. pieces.

Lay 12 slices of sourdough bread on a bread board and spread each one lightly with butter. Flip the slices and spread generously with Dijonnaise. Layer the bacon over the Dijonnaise and top with a couple of slices of the cured tomatoes.

Grate the 3 cheeses and mix together in a bowl. Pile a handful of the mixed cheeses on top of the bacon on each sandwich. Top with the remaining bread slices, Dijonnaise side down.

Place the sandwiches in an oven-safe frying pan/skillet in a preheated oven for a few minutes so the cheese melts nicely. Remove the sandwiches from the oven and let cool for 2 minutes before serving.

Traditionally, the Reuben sandwich is made with salt beef, but many delis are giving this classic sandwich a little makeover by using pastrami instead. They are similar cuts, but differently spiced, and while pastrami is made with beef shoulder, salt beef is made from brisket. There are a number of competing stories about who first invented the Reuben, but one thing's for sure – it's a New York staple.

pastrami Reuben on rye bread with homemade Russian dressing

for the Russian dressing

340 g/1½ cups mayonnaise

150 ml/⅔ cup chilli/chile sauce

75 g/⅓ cup sour cream

2 tablespoons horseradish sauce

1 tablespoon lemon juice

2 teaspoons sugar

2 teaspoons Worcestershire sauce

½ teaspoon hot sauce (page 56)

½ teaspoon paprika

1 dill pickle, chopped

1 spring onion/scallion, chopped

to assemble the sandwiches

225 g/1⅓ cup sauerkraut, drained and squeezed of moisture

8–16 slices Provolone cheese

8 slices rye bread

450 g/1 lb. pastrami, shaved

salted butter, softened, for spreading

salt and pepper to taste

Hand-cut Fries (page 113), to serve

makes **4**

To make the Russian dressing, mix all the ingredients in a food processor until combined. Season with salt and pepper to taste. Refrigerate.

Build the sandwich: mix half of the Russian dressing with the sauerkraut. Lay 4 slices of rye bread down and place 1–2 slices of Provolone cheese on each one, followed by a generous serving of pastrami and another 1–2 slices of cheese. Top with the sauerkraut mixture and a second piece of bread. Butter the outside of the sandwiches. Heat a griddle pan or a ridged stove-top pan over a low-medium heat. Add the sandwiches and grill for about 2–3 minutes per side, until the cheese has melted. Serve with hand-cut fries and extra Russian dressing on the side.

The posh fish finger sandwich is one of London's most famous dishes. Lager is often used in the batter for a richer flavour. Homemade tartare sauce and hand-cut fries finish the meal.

posh fish finger sandwich
& tartare sauce

2 skinned and boned fillets of cod or haddock

sunflower or vegetable oil, for frying

for the beer batter

200 g/1½ cups plain/all-purpose flour

2 teaspoons sea salt

2 x 330 ml/11 fl. oz. bottles of lager

for the homemade tartare sauce

225 g/1 cup mayonnaise

80 g/½ cup pickles/gherkins

1 teaspoon capers, chopped

2 teaspoons Dijon mustard

2 teaspoons chopped shallots

2 tablespoons spring onions/scallions, chopped

2 teaspoons lemon juice

Tabasco sauce to taste

sea salt and ground black pepper to taste

French Country Bread (page 28), to serve

butter, for spreading

handful of cos/romaine lettuce leaves, cut into strips, to serve

Hand-cut Fries (page 113), to serve

makes 2

Prepare your fish for battering. If the fish isn't already skinned and boned, do so. Slice the fish into a number of finger-size strips.

For the batter, whisk the flour, salt and lager in a bowl until combined.

Fill a large frying pan/skillet with about 2.5 cm/1 in. oil over a high heat, but don't leave this unattended. When the oil is bubbling steadily, it's ready to go. Dip the fish fingers in the batter, remove any excess and then lower carefully into the oil using tongs if necessary. Fry for about 4 minutes on each side over a moderate heat until golden and crispy.

Remove the fish fingers carefully from the oil and drain well on paper towels. Season with sea salt.

Mix all the ingredients for the tartare sauce together in a mixing bowl.

Cut the French Country Bread into thick slices. Lay one down and butter it before spreading a couple of tablespoons of tartare sauce on top. Place 3 fish fingers on top, then a few strips of lettuce, before placing a second slice of bread on top.

Serve with hand-cut fries.

Taking their name from the city in which they originated, Buffalo, New York, Buffalo wings have become an American staple, often served during sporting events or at late-night bars.

Buffalo bingo wings
with homemade ranch dressing

for the marinade

140 g/1 cup plain/all-purpose flour

½ teaspoon paprika

½ teaspoon cayenne pepper

½ teaspoon sea salt

20 chicken wings

for the ranch dressing

250 ml/1 cup buttermilk, shaken

60 g/¼ cup mayonnaise

3 tablespoons sour cream

3 tablespoons flat-leaf parsley, finely chopped

2 tablespoons chives, finely chopped

4 teaspoons white wine vinegar or lemon juice

1 garlic clove, finely chopped

¼ teaspoon garlic powder

½ teaspoon sea salt, plus extra if needed

2 pinches ground black pepper

for the hot sauce

½ cup butter

½ cup Louisiana hot sauce, or other hot pepper sauce

2 pinches ground black pepper

3 pinches garlic powder

vegetable oil, for frying

celery and carrots, for dipping

makes 20

Combine the flour, paprika, cayenne pepper and salt in a large resealable plastic bag. Shake the bag to combine the spices. Next, put the chicken wings in the bag, seal tightly and shake them to coat evenly in the spice mix. Place the bag in the refrigerator for 60–90 minutes.

Place all of the ranch dressing ingredients in a 500 ml/ 2 cup jar with a tight-fitting lid. Seal tightly and shake to evenly distribute all the ingredients. Taste and season with additional salt and pepper as desired. Refrigerate until chilled and the flavours have melded, about 1 hour. The dressing will last up to 3 days in the refrigerator.

Combine the butter, Louisiana or other hot pepper sauce, ground black pepper and garlic powder in a small saucepan over a low heat. Warm until the butter is melted and the ingredients are well blended. Set aside.

In a large, deep, frying pan/skillet, add the vegetable oil to a depth of 2.5–5 cm/1–2 in. and heat to 190°C (375°F) or until the oil is bubbling steadily. Alternatively, use a deep fryer and follow the manufacturer's instructions.

Put the wings into the heated oil and fry them for 10–15 minutes or until some parts of the wings begin to turn a golden to dark brown colour.

Remove the wings from the oil and drain on paper towels for a few seconds. Place the wings in a large bowl or in a large uncovered Tupperware box. Add the hot sauce mixture and stir, tossing the wings to thoroughly coat them.

Serve with the homemade ranch dressing and with a few sticks of celery and carrot.

There's chicken, and then there's marinaded, grilled, perfectly spiced, finger-lickin' chicken. This is that kind of chicken and its perfect partner has got to be Island-style Mac 'n' Cheese.

jerk chicken

1 tablespoon ground allspice

1 teaspoon dried thyme

1½ teaspoons cayenne pepper

1½ teaspoons ground black pepper

1½ teaspoons dried sage

¾ teaspoon ground nutmeg

¾ teaspoon ground cinnamon

1 tablespoon sugar

4 tablespoons olive oil

4 tablespoons soy sauce

175 ml/¾ cup white vinegar

125 ml/½ cup orange juice

freshly squeezed juice of 1 lime

1 Habanero or Scotch Bonnet chilli/chile pepper, deseeded and finely chopped

3 spring onions/scallions, finely chopped

120 g/1 cup onion, finely chopped

10 garlic cloves, minced

4–6 chicken breasts, or a whole chicken cut into pieces (skin left on)

Island-style Mac 'n' Cheese, to serve (page 74)

charcoal grill or barbecue

serves 4

Combine the first 8 ingredients in a large bowl.

Combine the olive oil, soy sauce, vinegar, orange juice and lime juice in a large measuring cup or small bowl. Slowly add the spice mixture, whisking it in until incorporated. Add the chilli/chile pepper, spring onions/scallions, onions and minced garlic and stir to finish the marinade.

Spread the marinade all over the chicken pieces. Place in a large resealable plastic bag and seal tightly. Refrigerate and marinate overnight, or for at least 4 hours.

When ready to cook, heat up either a barbecue or a charcoal grill.

Grill the chicken for about 6 minutes per side, brushing on more of the marinade while cooking and making sure that the marinade is well cooked (it will have been in contact with the raw chicken for several hours). Test if the chicken is cooked through by sticking a skewer in the thickest part – if the juices run clear, it is ready. Bring the leftover marinade to a fast boil for at least 4 minutes and serve as a dipping sauce.

Serve with mac 'n' cheese.

The first thing most people think of when they hear the term, "airline chicken" is a limp, sorry piece of chicken served as part of an in-flight meal on an aeroplane. This exciting, fruity dish is mercifully as far from that as you can get! It's actually named for how the chicken is butchered – a single breast with the first wing joint attached. Airline chicken is perfect for late-summer when blackberries are in season.

blackberry airline chicken

125 ml/½ cup chicken stock

1 tablespoon brown sugar

1 tablespoon white sugar

2 tablespoons white wine vinegar

1 teaspoon olive oil

3 garlic cloves, minced

¾ teaspoon paprika

4 airline chicken breasts (chicken breasts with ribs removed and wing intact)

1 sprig fresh thyme leaves, minced

½ teaspoon sea salt

¼ teaspoon ground black pepper

2–3 teaspoons cornflour/cornstarch

140 g/1 cup fresh blackberries

Creamed Corn & Bacon (page 117), to serve

French Country Bread (page 30), sliced, to serve

apple sauce, to serve

28 x 18 cm/11 x 7 in. baking pan coated with cooking spray or lightly greased with oil

serves 4

Preheat an oven to 190°C (375°F) Gas 5.

In a small mixing bowl, add half of the stock, both types of sugar, vinegar, oil, garlic, and a third of the paprika.

Place the chicken in the prepared baking dish and pour the stock mixture over the top. Sprinkle with the thyme, salt, pepper and the remaining paprika.

Bake in the preheated oven, uncovered, for 20–25 minutes, basting occasionally with pan juices. Remove the chicken and keep warm by covering with foil.

Skim the fat from the pan drippings and set the drippings aside. In a small saucepan, combine the cornflour/cornstarch and the remaining stock. Mix until the cornflour/cornstarch has dissolved then gradually stir in the pan drippings. Add three-quarters of the blackberries, mash them with a wooden spoon and bring the mixture to a boil. Cook and stir for 1–2 minutes or until this rich blackberry-based sauce thickens.

Serve the chicken on a bed of creamed corn, and pour over a little of the warm blackberry sauce and homemade apple sauce. Sprinkle the remaining blackberries on top if desired. Soak up the sauces with thick slices of French country bread.

Fried chicken is one of the world's most popular foods and each culture has their own version. Some like buttermilk-fried chicken, some prefer extra-crispy, double fried chicken and others, particularly in the American south with a sweet tooth, prefer this delicious honey-fried version.

honey-fried chicken

1 x 1.8 kg/4 lbs. whole chicken, cut into pieces

sea salt and ground black pepper to taste

170 g/½ cup runny honey

1 tablespoon garlic powder

1 x 4 g cube/⅙ oz. packet chicken bouillon granules

260 g/2 cups plain/all-purpose flour

1 litre/quart vegetable oil, for frying

Creamed Corn (page 117), to serve

serves 4

Season chicken pieces with salt and pepper, then coat each seasoned chicken piece with honey.

In a shallow dish or bowl, mix together the garlic powder, chicken bouillon granules and flour. Dredge the honey-coated chicken pieces in the flour mixture, coating completely.

Fill a large, heavy-bottomed frying-pan/skillet with oil to a depth of 2.5 cm/1 in. and heat over a medium-high heat until the oil is bubbling steadily.

In batches, fry the chicken for at least 8 minutes per side, until it's no longer pink and until the juices run clear. Make sure you heat the oil back up so it's bubbling steadily before frying the next batch.

Serve with creamed corn and enjoy!

Everyone has their own preference when it comes to BBQ ribs. Some like them rubbed with spices with no sauce, while others smother sauce over the top. Chicago-style ribs involve both a rub and a sauce; for best results they're first grilled slowly then cooked in the oven to make them really tender.

Chicago-style baby back ribs

2 racks of baby back ribs

for the dry rub

1 tablespoon paprika

1 teaspoon celery salt

1 teaspoon dark brown sugar

1 teaspoon garlic powder

1/4 teaspoon mustard powder

1/4 teaspoon dried thyme

1/4 teaspoon ground white pepper

1/4 teaspoon cayenne pepper

for the BBQ sauce

340 g/2 1/2 cups tomato ketchup

115 g/1/2 cup golden
syrup/molasses

125 ml/1/2 cup apple cider vinegar

125 ml/1/2 cup water

1 teaspoon granulated sugar

1/2 teaspoon salt

1/2 teaspoon ground black pepper

charcoal grill or barbecue

Mix the dry rub ingredients together in a bowl. Rub the ribs with the spice mix and let sit for 30 minutes.

Preheat a charcoal grill or barbecue. Cook the ribs over an indirect medium heat for 10–15 minutes.

Preheat an oven to 120°C (250°F) Gas 1/2.

Add about 1.25 cm/1/2 in water to an oblong baking pan and place a grill rack into the pan. Place the ribs on the rack and cover tightly with foil. Bake for approximately 1 1/2 hours and remove from the oven.

Mix all the sauce ingredients together in a cup and spread over the ribs, reserving some to serve. Cover tightly again with foil and set aside for 15 minutes before serving. Serve along with the extra sauce.

BBQ specialities vary greatly across the US. In Memphis, Tennessee, they slather BBQ sauce on their pork and use it as a baster, while Carolina-style involves BBQ pork with a mustard sauce, inspired by early German settlers in that region. Kansas City BBQ uses a wide range of meat, which is slowly smoked, while in Texas, beef alone is king.

Texas-style brisket

for the dry rub

2 tablespoons chilli powder

2 tablespoons sea salt

1 tablespoon garlic powder

1 tablespoon cayenne pepper

1/2 teaspoon dried oregano

1 tablespoon onion powder

1 tablespoon ground black pepper

1 tablespoons brown sugar

2 teaspoons dry mustard

1 fresh bay leaf, crushed

1.8 kg/4 lbs. beef brisket, trimmed

375 ml/1 1/2 cups beef stock

Rosemary Coleslaw (page 110), to serve

serves 4–6

Preheat an oven to 180°C (350°F) Gas 4.

Combine all the dry rub ingredients together in a bowl. Season the raw brisket on both sides with the rub. Place the brisket in a roasting pan and roast in the preheated oven, uncovered, for 1 hour.

Add the beef stock and enough water so that there is about 1.25 cm/1/2 in. of liquid in the roasting pan. Reduce the oven temperature to 150°C (350°F) Gas 2, cover the pan tightly and continue cooking for 3 hours, or until fork-tender.

Remove the brisket from the oven. Trim any fat away from the brisket and slice the meat thinly across the grain. Top with a little juice from the pan and reserve the rest of the drippings, along with any leftover brisket, to prepare Burnt Ends (page 68). Serve with rosemary coleslaw.

Burnt Ends are the pieces of meat cut from the narrower end of a brisket, and they are considered a delicacy in southern cooking. Although Burnt Ends are mainly associated with Kansas City BBQ, many other BBQ cultures have adopted it. The high fat content of the brisket point takes longer to cook to tender, hence the term 'Burnt Ends'. In this version, it is served on a bun with a side of Island Mac and Cheese and Sweet Potato Fries.

burnt ends

1 cooked beef brisket (page 67)

125–250 ml/½–1 cup BBQ sauce (page 64)

125 ml/½ cup drippings from smoked brisket, reserved

4 Pretzel Buns (page 29)

Sweet Potato Fries (page 114), to serve

Island Mac 'n' Cheese (page 74), to serve

food smoker or barbecue

serves 4

Cut the brisket into 1.25 cm/½ in. cubes and place in a large disposable tray. Add in the BBQ sauce and brisket drippings. Toss thoroughly.

Prepare a smoker following the manufacturer's instructions. If you haven't got a smoker, use a barbecue smoker box and fill it with wood chips that have been soaked in water or fruit juice for a couple of hours. Place the smoker box directly into a lit charcoal or gas barbecue.

Place the tray in the smoker or barbecue and smoke at 100°C (225°F) until the brisket pieces darken and become crisp around the edges, 30–45 minutes.

Remove from the smoker or barbecue, and set aside to let cool for 10 minutes.

Serve on a bun with additional BBQ sauce, if desired, alongside sweet potato fries and mac 'n' cheese.

This unconventional take on the classic pork and apple combination is quick to prepare and really tasty. It brings together cinnamon, ginger, garlic and soy sauce for a rich and sweet mix of flavours. It goes well with an Ice Box Salad (page 86) and thick slices of French Country Bread (page 28).

pork chops & baked apple

4 medium apples, peeled, cored and cubed

175 ml/³/4 cup water

130 g/²/3 cup granulated sugar

¹/2 teaspoon ground cinnamon

1 tablespoon soy sauce

1 garlic clove, minced

¹/4 teaspoon ground ginger

2 tablespoons butter, for frying

4 boneless pork chops, 1.25 cm/ ¹/2 in. thick

casserole or baking dish, greased

makes 4

In a saucepan over a medium heat, combine the apples, water, sugar, cinnamon, soy sauce, garlic and ginger. Stir well with a wooden spoon and cook, covered, for 15–20 minutes, or until the apples are soft.

Prepare the baking dish.

Heat the butter up in a large frying pan/skillet over a medium heat and braise the pork chops, browning each side for about 5 minutes per side.

Pour the apples and sauce into the casserole or baking dish and arrange the pork chops on top.

Bake, uncovered for 20–30 minutes or until the meat is tender and serve immediately.

Macaroni and cheese is one of the most popular meals and side dishes around the world. This recipe adds a little kick with the addition of cayenne pepper, mustard and nutmeg, while Greek yogurt reduces the richness slightly without losing the taste.

island mac 'n' cheese

240 g/2 cups macaroni, cooked al dente

450 g/1 lb. Cheddar cheese, half cubed, half grated/shredded

225 g/½ lb. Monterey pepper jack cheese or Gouda, cubed

2 teaspoons plain/all-purpose flour

½ teaspoon salt

½ teaspoon ground black pepper

1 teaspoon cayenne pepper

½ teaspoon dry mustard

pinch of ground nutmeg

¼ finely grated white onion

½ green (bell) pepper, minced

1 large (UK), extra large (US) egg, beaten

4 tablespoons sour cream or Greek yogurt

300 ml/1¼ cups double/heavy cream mixed with 60 ml/¼ cup whole milk

4 slices of day-old bread

yellow mustard, to serve

serves 6

Preheat the oven to 180°C (350°F) Gas 4.

In a large bowl, toss together the cooked pasta with the cheese cubes and pour into either a large baking dish or a casserole dish.

In a separate large bowl, mix together the flour, salt, black pepper, cayenne pepper, dry mustard, nutmeg, onion, green (bell) pepper, egg, double/heavy cream and milk. Pour this mixture over the pasta and cover with the grated/shredded Cheddar. Bake uncovered until the top is just beginning to brown, about 30 minutes.

Meanwhile, cut the bread into crouton-size squares. Sprinkle these cubes on top of the macaroni and cheese and bake until golden brown, about 15 minutes more.

Every family has a treasured recipe that has been passed down the generations and brings back wonderful memories. This recipe is one of those, adapted from my Grandma Stella's spaghetti sauce recipe.

Stella's spaghetti & meatballs

for the spaghetti sauce

90 g/^{3}/$_4$ cup chopped onion

6 cloves garlic, minced

50 g/^{1}/$_4$ cup extra-virgin olive oil

2 x 400-g/14-oz. cans whole, peeled tomatoes

2 teaspoons sea salt

1 teaspoon granulated sugar

1 fresh bay leaf

170 g/6 oz. tomato purée/paste

^{3}/$_4$ teaspoon dried basil

^{1}/$_2$ teaspoon ground black pepper

for the meatballs

2 tablespoons extra-virgin olive oil

225 g/^{1}/$_2$ lb. lean minced/ground beef

225 g/^{1}/$_2$ lb. ground thin/short rib

1 cup fresh bread crumbs

1 tablespoons dried parsley

2 tablespoons Parmesan cheese, grated

^{1}/$_4$ teaspoon ground black pepper

pinch of garlic powder

1 egg, beaten

500 g/1^1/$_8$ lbs. dried spaghetti

salt, to taste

serves 4

For the spaghetti sauce, in a large saucepan over a medium heat, sauté the onion and garlic in olive oil until the onion is translucent. Stir in the tomatoes, salt, sugar and bay leaf. Cover the saucepan and reduce the heat to low. Simmer for 1–1^1/$_2$ hours. Stir in the tomato purée/paste, basil and black pepper. Refrigerate until ready to use.

Preheat an oven to 190°C (375°F) Gas 5.

For the meatballs, combine all ingredients well in a mixing bowl with your hands and form into golf-ball size balls. Place on a baking sheet and transfer to the preheated oven for 20 minutes. Use immediately or turn out onto a plate to cool and then place them in a resealable plastic bag in the freezer.

Bring a pot of salted water to a boil and add the spaghetti. When the spaghetti reaches an al dente texture, about 8–10 minutes, remove and drain. Mix with the sauce, add the meatballs and finish by adding a generous sprinkling of freshly grated Parmesan cheese.

To make in a slow-cooker, set the heat to its lowest setting and cook the meatballs and sauce for 6–8 hours. Follow the above directions for cooking the spaghetti.

This recipe is inspired by the famous Jacques Pépin, one of the world's most acclaimed chefs. The tomato, goat's cheese and mushroom flavours intertwine for a hearty, yet elegant meal. Like every pasta, after a few days in the refrigerator, the flavours intensify, making this dish better with every passing day.

Parisian gnocchi

for the roasted tomato sauce

50 g/¼ cup olive oil

1 x 800-g/28-oz. can whole plum tomatoes

225 g/½ lb. mushrooms, cut and sliced

½ medium onion, sliced

6 cloves of garlic, minced

¼ teaspoon chilli/hot red pepper flakes

3 teaspoons fresh oregano, chopped

sea salt and ground black pepper to taste

for the gnocchi

250 ml/1 cup water

1 teaspoon sea salt

pinch of black pepper

¼ teaspoon fresh nutmeg, grated

3 tablespoons unsalted butter

140 g/1 cup plain/all-purpose flour

3 large eggs

3 tablespoons Gruyere cheese, grated/shredded

4 tablespoons goat's cheese, cubed, to serve

handful of toasted pumpkin seeds, to serve

2 x 33 x 23 cm/13 x 9 in. baking dishes

serves 4

Preheat an oven to 210°C (425°F) Gas 7.

Firstly, make the roasted tomato sauce. Drizzle the olive oil over the bottom of 33 x 23 cm/13 x 9 in. baking dish. Slice each tomato into 3 pieces and add them to the dish along with the tomato juice from the can. Add the mushrooms, onion, garlic, chilli/hot red pepper flakes and 2 teaspoons of oregano. Stir to combine and add salt and pepper to taste. Roast in the preheated oven for 1 hour.

Meanwhile, make the gnocchi. In a small saucepan over a high heat, combine the water, salt, pepper and nutmeg with 2 tablespoons of the butter and bring to a boil. Add the flour all at once and beat the dough with a wooden spoon until it's thick and it comes away from the sides of the pan. Keep the mixture moving to avoid burning it. Cook, stirring to dry out the dough for about 30 seconds. Transfer the dough to a medium bowl and allow to cool for 5 minutes.

Bring a large pot of salted water to the boil over high heat. Set a medium bowl of iced water near the stove.

Beat an egg into the dough until it's been fully incorporated, then beat in 1 tablespoon of the cheese and another egg until well blended. Beat in the last egg until the dough is smooth and shiny. With a spatula, transfer the dough to a large, resealable plastic bag or pastry bag, pressing it into one corner. Cut the tip off of the bag to create an opening about 1.25 cm/½ in. wide.

Once the water has come to the boil, reduce to a simmer. Over a wooden chopping board, squeeze out the dough into 1.25 cm/½ in. lengths and cut with a small knife. Transfer the gnocchi to the water and simmer for 3 minutes. Remove with a slotted spoon and dip the gnocchi in the iced water quickly before patting them dry with paper towels.

Grease another 33 x 23 cm/13 x 9 in. baking dish with the remaining butter. Scatter the gnocchi into the dish and sprinkle with the remaining cheese. Bake in the preheated oven until puffed up, about 25 minutes.

Meanwhile, remove the roasted tomatoes from the oven, stir briefly, return to the oven and continue to roast for an additional 10–15 minutes. Transfer the roasted tomato mixture into a saucepan. Pour in a little water and process the mixture with a handheld blender or potato masher until the desired consistency is reached. Stir in the last teaspoon of oregano. Season with salt and black pepper to taste and set aside.

Preheat a grill/broiler. Remove the gnocchi from the oven and grill/broil it 15 cm/6 in. from the heat until browned, about 1–2 minutes.

Heat up the roasted tomato sauce if needed and pour it over the gnocchi and stir to combine. Sprinkle the goat's cheese cubes over the top and scatter over a few toasted pumpkin seeds.

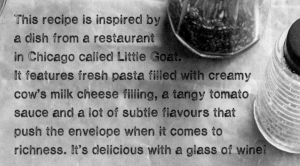

This recipe is inspired by a dish from a restaurant in Chicago called Little Goat. It features fresh pasta filled with creamy cow's milk cheese filling, a tangy tomato sauce and a lot of subtle flavours that push the envelope when it comes to richness. It's delicious with a glass of wine!

ricotta & mortadella ravioli

for the homemade pasta

260 g/2 cups plain/all-purpose flour

2 eggs

1 tablespoon extra-virgin olive oil

4 tablespoons water

for the ravioli filling

675 g/1½ lbs. creamy cow's milk cheese

115 g/¼ lb. sheep's milk ricotta

2 eggs, beaten lightly

55 g/2 oz. mortadella, finely chopped

pinch of ground nutmeg

sea salt and ground black pepper, to taste

Roasted Tomato Sauce (page 78), to serve

Parmesan cheese, finely grated/shredded, to serve

sea salt and ground black pepper, to serve

pasta roller

pizza cutter

serves 4

To make the pasta, add all the ingredients (but only half the water) to a food processor. Process into a ball. Add the second half of the water after the mixture just starts to come together. Wrap the ball in clingfilm/plastic wrap and let rest for about 1 hour at room temperature. If it's hot where you live, place the ball of pasta dough in the refrigerator.

Meanwhile, make the Roasted Tomato Sauce (page 78).

Divide the pasta dough into quarters and, using a pasta roller, roll each section of the dough into rectangles approximately 4mm/⅙ in. thick and set aside.

To make the ravioli filling, in a mixing bowl, combine all the ingredients well with your hands and set to the side.

Lay out 2 sheets of the rolled-out pasta dough. Carefully place 1–1½ teaspoons of the filling at intervals of about 4 cm/1½ in. apart all along the dough.

Cover the filling with the other 2 sheets of the dough. Using your fingers, gently press the dough between each dab of filling to seal it.

Using a pizza cutter, cut the dough into squares, with the now-covered filling forming the centre of each square.

Allow the ravioli to dry at room temperature for about 1 hour before cooking.

Bring 7.5 litres/8 quarts of salted water to the boil over a medium-high heat. Cook until the ravioli is tender, about 3–4 minutes. Remove the ravioli from the pot carefully with a large slotted spoon. Drain well.

Place the drained ravioli on a serving platter, alternating pasta layers with layers of roasted tomato sauce. Serve hot and sprinkle with Parmesan, salt and ground black pepper.

Linguiça is the Bentley of sausages. It's a form of pork sausage smoked over oak for hours, usually accompanied by onion and garlic. Adding it to a gumbo contributes an extra richness and depth to this flavoursome Deep South-inspired dish.

Portuguese linguiça gumbo

8 thin Portuguese linguiça sausages or chorizo, chopped

3 tablespoons olive oil

1 small green (bell) pepper, diced

2 stalks celery, diced

½ large vidalia or yellow onion, diced

5 cloves garlic, minced

Cajun seasoning, to taste

2 tablespoons plain/all-purpose flour

4 roma or plum tomatoes, chopped

1 fresh bay leaf

1 fresh thyme sprig, leaves only, chopped

500 ml/2 cups chicken stock

200 g/3 cups okra, sliced

handful fresh flat-leaf parsley, chopped, to serve

ground black pepper, to serve

long-grain rice, to serve (optional)

serves 4

Add the olive oil to a heavy cooking pot with a tight-fitting lid over a medium-high heat. After the oil has heated up, add the sausages and cook until they brown, around 5 minutes. Remove the sausages from the heat and set aside.

Add the green (bell) pepper, celery and onion to the same pot as you used to cook the sausages, adding more oil if necessary, and cook, stirring often, until the onion becomes translucent, about 2 minutes. Add garlic and Cajun seasoning and cook, stirring often, until fragrant, about 30 seconds. Add the flour and cook, continuously stirring to coat the vegetables, until the flour browns, about 1 minute. Add the tomatoes, bay leaf and thyme and cook, stirring occasionally, until they begin to release their juices, about 2 minutes. Stir in the chicken stock, increase the heat to high and bring to the boil.

Return the sausages to the pan, cover with the lid, and reduce the heat to a simmer for approximately 1 hour. Add the okra for the last 15 minutes. Serve sprinkled with flat-leaf parsley, ground black pepper and long-grain rice, if desired.

Beef Stroganoff is not traditionally a sexy dish. It's beef, noodles and mushrooms. But over the years, this hearty meal has reinvented itself. This version makes a fitting meal for anything from a Tuesday night to Valentine's Day.

beef Stroganoff

4 pieces beef chuck thin short ribs, (cut across the bone), about 450 g/1 lb. each

3 tablespoons vegetable oil

sea salt and ground black pepper to taste

2 medium carrots, chopped

1 medium yellow onion, diced

1 litre/4 cups beef stock

1 x 70 cl/24 fl. oz. bottle dry red wine

handful fresh flat-leaf parsley, chopped

2 stalks fresh tarragon

2 fresh bay leaves

few sprigs fresh thyme

1 tablespoon unsalted butter

2 tablespoons sour cream

2 pinches ground nutmeg

1 tablespoon grain mustard

handful dried porcini mushrooms,

500 g/18 oz. pappardelle pasta

handful of fresh flat-leaf parsley, chopped, to garnish

coarse sea salt and freshly ground black pepper, to serve

cooking twine

serves 4

Preheat an oven to 200°C (400°F) Gas 6.

Season the meat with salt and pepper. Tie the ribs tightly around the bone with 3 separate loops of cooking twine.

Place the ribs in a large, deep casserole dish. Heat 2 tablespoons of vegetable oil over a high heat until it starts to shimmer. Reduce the heat to medium-high and use tongs to add the ribs. Turn them over carefully using the tongs to brown on all sides.

Take the ribs out of the oven and place on a plate. In the same casserole dish add another tablespoon of oil. Add the carrots and onion and cook until caramelized, about 5 minutes, stirring occasionally. Add the beef stock and red wine, parsley, tarragon, bay leaves and thyme and bring to a boil. Carefully place the rolled ribs into the braising liquid. Add more beef stock if necessary so that the beef is covered in liquid. Place a tight-fitting lid on top.

Put the casserole dish in the preheated oven and cook for 2½ hours. Take the dish out of the oven and use a slotted spoon to remove the vegetables. Take the ribs out and set aside. Over a high heat, reduce the liquid for a few minutes. Add the butter, sour cream, nutmeg, mustard and porcini mushrooms to the reduced sauce and turn the heat down.

Meanwhile, bring a large saucepan of water to the boil, add the pappardelle, turn down the heat slightly and cook the pasta for 10–12 minutes. Drain and stir in some butter to the pasta with a wooden spoon.

Place the ribs back in the sauce and baste. Remember to remove the cooking twine.

To serve, spoon a quarter of the pappardelle onto four plates and lay a piece of beef down; drizzle some of the sauce on top, add salt and pepper to taste and garnish with parsley.

Often served at BBQs, picnics and bring-a-dish parties, the Icebox Salad tastes even better after a few hours in the refrigerator, making this a great dish to make in advance. The top layers of chopped vegetables keep the dressing from soaking the layer of lettuce. As time passes, the dressing infuses sweetness into the peas, radishes and cucumbers.

ice-box salad

200 g/7 oz. assorted lettuce (my favourite is an iceberg, butterhead and cos/romaine trio)

1 cucumber, chopped into small cubes

6–8 radishes, sliced thinly

340 g/³/₄ lb. sugar-snap peas, coarsely chopped

170–225 g/ 1¼–1³/₄ oz. frozen peas (leave frozen)

1 bunch spring onions/scallions, chopped

1 batch Homemade Ranch Dressing (page 56)

250 g/9 oz. grated/shredded Parmesan cheese or other hard cheese

stainless steel roasting pan

serves 4–6

In a stainless steel roasting pan, layer the lettuce, cucumber, radishes, sugar-snap peas, frozen peas and spring onions/scallions. Drizzle the ranch dressing over the top until the vegetables are completely covered. Top with grated/ shredded Parmesan. Chill for 2–6 hours, then enjoy!

This dish hails from an area in the US known as the Lowcountry, comprising parts of South Carolina and Georgia. Lowcountry cuisine is a melting pot of influences and incorporates a wide range of ingredients, from the sophisticated and expensive to the unashamedly basic. This dish embodies this spectrum. Grits are common in the US, while in the UK, they can be found in some larger supermarkets, as well as through online suppliers.

fried oysters & grits

200 g/1 cup grits

500 ml/2 cups whole milk

sea salt, to taste

ground black pepper, to taste

canola oil, for frying

16 oysters, shucked and cleaned

360 g/3 cups flour

500 ml/2 cups buttermilk

Tabasco sauce, to serve

serves 4

Add the grits and milk to a small saucepan and bring to the boil, then turn the heat down and simmer until the grits are fully cooked, about 30 minutes. Add milk or water as needed if the grits get too dry. Season with salt and pepper and keep warm.

Set 7.5 cm/3 in. of canola oil in a medium frying pan/skillet over a medium-high heat (or use a deep fryer and follow the manufacturer's instructions). Set up 2 medium bowls, one containing the flour and the other with the buttermilk. Bring the oil to 160°C (325°F), or until it is bubbling steadily. Roll the oysters in the flour and then dip them in the buttermilk. Shake off excess flour, and repeat the rolling and dipping process one more time. Fry the oysters until they're golden-brown, about 1 minute. Season with salt and drain on paper towels.

Divide the grits and the oysters among 4 bowls and serve along with a dash of Tabasco sauce, if desired.

There is something so satisfying about an egg roll. Maybe it's the crunch; maybe it's the texture; maybe it's something about how pork and cabbage come together so well when hugged between egg roll wrappers and deep fried. Whatever it is, they're delicious!

egg rolls

3 tablespoons olive oil

1 teaspoon sea salt

1 teaspoon ground black pepper

1 teaspoon ground ginger

1 teaspoon garlic powder

450 g/1 lb. pork shoulder

1 litre/quart peanut oil, for frying

2 tablespoons plain/all-purpose flour

2 tablespoons water

120 g/2 cups cabbage, shredded

1 medium carrot, shredded

8 x 18-cm/7-in square egg roll wrappers

2 tablespoons sesame seeds (optional)

for the sweet and sour sauce

1 tablespoon soy sauce

1 tablespoon water

3 1/2 tablespoons sugar

3 1/2 tablespoons white vinegar

zest of 1 unwaxed orange

meat thermometer

makes 8

Preheat an oven to 180°C (350°F) Gas 4.

Spread the oil, salt, ground black pepper, ginger and garlic powder on the pork shoulder.

Set the meat on a rack set into a roasting pan. Roast for 20 minutes, and then reduce the heat to 160°C (325°F) Gas 3. Continue to cook until an instant-read thermometer inserted into the shoulder reads 85°C (185°F), about 1–2 hours. Remove the pork from the oven and let stand until cool enough to handle, about 30 minutes. Shred the pork.

Combine the flour and water in a bowl until they form a paste. In a separate bowl combine the cabbage, carrots and shredded pork and mix them together.

Lay out one egg roll wrapper with a corner pointed toward you. Place about 20 g/1/4 cup of the cabbage, carrot and shredded pork mixture onto the wrapper and fold the corner up over the mixture. Fold the left and right corners toward the centre and continue to roll. Brush a bit of the flour paste on the final corner to help seal.

In a large frying pan/skillet, heat the peanut oil to about 190°C (375°F). Place the egg rolls into the heated oil and fry, turning occasionally, until golden brown. Remove from oil and drain on paper towels or a wire rack. Put on a serving plate and top with sesame seeds if desired.

To make the sweet and sour sauce, mix all the ingredients together in a mixing bowl. Transfer to a small saucepan and bring to the boil, then remove from the heat. Pour the sauce into a small bowl ready to dip the egg rolls into.

If the **Vietnamese** spring roll had a song, it would probably be "Say My Name" by Destiny's Child. There are so many names for the ever-popular spring roll, including salad roll, summer roll and crystal roll, although there might be parts of the world where trying to buy a "crystal roll" just might land you in jail. Or rehab.

Vietnamese spring rolls

55 g/2 oz. rice vermicelli

8 rice wrappers (21.5 cm/8½ in. diameter)

4–6 shiitake mushrooms, cut into matchstick pieces

115 g/½ cup medium to firm tofu, sliced into matchstick pieces

30 g/½ cup cabbage, shredded or finely chopped

1⅓ tablespoons fresh Thai basil, chopped

3 tablespoons fresh mint leaves, chopped

3 tablespoons fresh coriander/cilantro, chopped

2 lettuce leaves of choice, chopped

4 teaspoons fish sauce

60 ml/¼ cup water

2 tablespoons freshly squeezed lime juice

1 clove garlic, minced

2 tablespoons white sugar

½ teaspoon garlic chilli/chile sauce

3 tablespoons hoisin sauce

1 teaspoon peanuts, finely chopped

makes 8

Bring a medium saucepan of water to boil. Boil the rice vermicelli for 3–5 minutes, or until al dente, and drain.

Fill a large bowl with warm water. Dip one rice wrapper into the hot water for 1 second to soften. Lay the wrapper flat. In a row across the centre of the wrapper, place 1 tablespoon of shiitake, 1 tablespoon tofu, a handful of cabbage, basil, mint, coriander/cilantro and lettuce, leaving about 5 cm/2 in. uncovered on each side. Fold the uncovered sides inward, then tightly roll the wrapper, beginning at the end with the lettuce. Repeat to make another 7 spring rolls.

In a small bowl, mix the fish sauce, water, lime juice, garlic, sugar and garlic chilli/chile sauce. In another small bowl, mix the hoisin sauce and peanuts.

Serve the spring rolls at room temperature and dip them into both sauces at will!

This dish combines two delicious dishes that are just too hard to choose between in a Chinese restaurant!

sweet & sour orange chicken

for the chicken

675 g/1½ lbs boneless skinless chicken, chopped into bite-sized pieces

2 eggs

1 teaspoon salt

ground white pepper to taste

1 litre/quart peanut oil, for frying

40 g/⅓ cup cornflour/cornstarch, plus 1 tablespoon for thickening

35 g/¼ cup plain/all-purpose flour

4 rings fresh (or canned) pineapple, drained (juice reserved)

1 tablespoon ginger, minced

1 teaspoon garlic, minced

2 green (bell) peppers, in small pieces

½ tablespoon chilli/hot red pepper flakes

¼ cup chopped spring onion/scallion

1 tablespoon rice wine

Sweet & Sour Sauce (page 92), to serve

60 ml/¼ cup water

for the pineapple fried rice

8 rings fresh (or canned) pineapple, drained

2 tablespoons canola oil

1 teaspoon garlic, minced

1 teaspoon ginger, minced

½ yellow onion, chopped

1 red (bell) pepper, chopped

½ carrot, grated

240 g/2 cups cooked rice

1–2 tablespoons light soy sauce

1 teaspoon Madras curry powder

sugar, to taste

1 spring onion/scallion, chopped

serves 4

For the orange chicken, place the chicken pieces in a large bowl. Be sure to handle raw chicken with care.

In another large bowl, stir together the eggs, salt, pepper and 1 tablespoon of the peanut oil. Mix well.

In a small bowl, whisk 40 g/⅓ cup cornflour/cornstarch and flour together. Mix the flour mixture into egg mixture. Add the chicken pieces, tossing to coat.

Heat the rest of the peanut oil in a large frying pan/skillet, wok or deep-fryer to 190°C (375°F) or until the oil is bubbling steadily. Add the chicken pieces, a few at a time. Fry for 3–4 minutes or until golden crisp.

Remove the chicken from the oil with a slotted spoon; drain on paper towels then set aside. Clean the wok or frying pan/skillet and heat for 15 seconds over a high heat. Add a little oil and then add the ginger and garlic. Stir-fry for 10 seconds or until fragrant. Add the peppers, chilli/hot red pepper flakes, spring onions/scallions, and rice wine. Stir for a few seconds. Add the sweet and sour sauce and bring to the boil. Add the cooked chicken, stirring until well mixed.

Stir water into the remaining 1 tablespoon cornflour/cornstarch until smooth and add to the chicken. Heat until the sauce has thickened and then turn off the gas.

To make the pineapple fried rice, cut the pineapple rings into small wedges. Heat a wok or frying pan/skillet over a medium to medium-high heat. Add the oil, rotating the pan so that it coats the bottom and sides.

When the oil is hot, add the garlic and ginger. Stir-fry for 30 seconds. Add the onion. Stir-fry for 1 minute, then add the red (bell) pepper, grated carrot and pineapple. Mix everything together and then add the rice and cook for 2 minutes. Stir the mixture and toss in the pan until it looks shiny. Add the soy sauce and stir in. Stir in the curry powder and sugar. Taste and adjust the seasoning if desired. Stir in the spring onion/scallion or use as a garnish.

This rich, creamy curry can be made as mild or as spicy as you like by adjusting the cayenne pepper. "Makhani" is a Hindustani word translating as "with butter", giving rise to its other more common name in the West – butter chicken.

chicken makhani

2 tablespoons peanut oil

1 shallot, finely chopped

¼ white onion, chopped

2 tablespoons butter

2 teaspoons lemon juice

1 tablespoon ginger-garlic paste

2 teaspoons garam masala

1 teaspoon chilli powder

1 teaspoon ground cumin

1 fresh bay leaf

200 g/1 cup strained tomatoes

(UK) 120 ml double cream and 120 ml whole milk, mixed, or (US) 1 cup half and half

55 g/¼ cup plain Greek yogurt

sea salt and ground black pepper, to taste

¼ teaspoon cayenne pepper, or to taste

1 pound boneless, skinless chicken thighs, cut into bite-size pieces

1 teaspoon garam masala

1 pinch cayenne pepper

1 tablespoon cornstarch/cornflour

60 ml/¼ cup water

white rice, to serve

naan bread, to serve

serves 4

Heat 1 tablespoon of peanut oil in a large saucepan over a medium-high heat. Sauté the shallot and onion until soft and translucent. Stir in butter, lemon juice, ginger-garlic paste, 1 teaspoon garam masala, chilli powder, cumin and the bay leaf. Cook, stirring frequently, for 1 minute. Add the strained tomatoes and cook for another 2 minutes, continuing to stir frequently. Stir in the cream mixture/half-and-half and add the Greek yogurt. Reduce the heat to low, and simmer for 10 minutes, stirring frequently. Season with salt and pepper. Remove from heat and set aside.

Heat the rest of the oil in a large, heavy frying pan/skillet over a medium heat. Add the chicken once the oil is hot and cook until lightly browned, about 10 minutes. Reduce the heat, and season with the rest of the garam masala and cayenne pepper to taste. Stir in a few spoonfuls of the sauce, and simmer until the liquid has reduced, and until the chicken is no longer pink. Stir the rest of the sauce into the cooked chicken.

In a bowl, mix together the cornflour/cornstarch and water, then stir into the chicken and sauce. Cook for 5–10 minutes, or until thickened.

Serve with white rice and naan bread.

Aloo pies are a Trinidadian variant of the samosa, the triangular filled pastries that originated in Uttar Pradesh in India. This easy-to-make-at-home pie is filled with beef, potatoes, spices and bags of flavour.

Trinidadian aloo pies

for the pastry

280 g/2 cups plain/all-purpose flour, plus extra for dusting

2 teaspoons baking powder

1/2 teaspoon salt

175 ml/3/4 cup water

for the filling

450 g/1 lb. beef stew meat or thin/short rib (cut into cubes)

875 ml/3 1/2 cups water

1 teaspoon salt

1 teaspoon ground black pepper

1 teaspoon ketchup

1 spring onion/scallion

2–3 tablespoons chopped coriander/cilantro

1 medium tomato, diced

3 tablespoons vegetable oil

1 onion, sliced

3 cloves garlic, minced

1/2 hot chilli/chile pepper, deseeded

1 tablespoon Madras curry powder

1/4 teaspoon ground cumin

3 medium potatoes, quartered

1 litre/quart vegetable oil, for frying

serves 4

To make the dough, mix the flour, baking powder, salt and water and knead lightly. Set aside, covered with a bowl or a wet cloth.

Add the cubed beef to a mixing bowl and season with salt and black pepper; add the ketchup, spring onion/scallion, coriander/cilantro and tomato. Then cover and place in the refrigerator to marinate for 2 hours. If you're in a rush, marinate for at least 15 minutes.

After marinating, put a frying pan/skillet on a medium heat and allow the 3 tablespoons of oil to get really hot. Add the onion, garlic and hot chilli/chile pepper and allow to cook until you start seeing the edges go golden brown. This is an indication that it's time to add the curry powder and ground cumin. Cook for 1–2 minutes, then add 60 ml/1/4 cup of water. Cook for another 5 minutes so that the liquid burns off and you're left with a sort of grainy paste on the bottom of the pan/skillet. Add the beef at this point and stir well. Cover the pan/skillet, turn down the heat to low and allow this to cook for 25–35 minutes.

Meanwhile, peel, wash and cube the potato, add the remaining water and place it in a bowl.

After the beef mixture has been cooking for 25–35 minutes, remove the lid and turn up the heat to burn off any remaining liquid. Add the potato and water, bring to a boil and reduce to a gentle simmer. Ensure the pan is covered and cook for about 40–50 minutes, until the beef is really tender and most of the liquid is gone. If you find that the liquid is still runny and the beef is tender, simply turn the heat up and cook until you get to the desired thickness. Taste and season again if desired. Set aside.

On a dusted floured work surface, divide the dough into 8 balls. Flatten these balls into 10-cm/4-in. diameter circles with a rolling pin and spread out the beef and potato mixture over one half of the circle. Seal by folding the other half of the dough circle over the top. Wet the edges with water and close and pinch shut tightly.

Heat up 1 litre/quart of oil in a frying pan/skillet over a medium heat to about 190°C (375°F) or until the oil starts bubbling steadily. Add the aloo pies until they turn golden brown, about 2 minutes. Carefully flip them over and fry them on the other side for another 2 minutes. Remove the pies and drain with paper towels before cutting them down the middle and spooning the beef curry over.

To most people, falafel is the sort of treat that can be enjoyed without remorse or shame. It is the perfect combination of good and bad. The good side is that it's made with chickpeas, it's low in fat, and it's filling and delicious. The bad side is that it's fried, but this isn't exactly a healthy food cookbook, so enjoy!

falafel

500 ml/2¼ cups dried chickpeas

1 medium onion, quartered

2 teaspoons salt

pinch ground black pepper

2–3 garlic cloves

2–3 slices stale bread

3 tablespoons fresh flat-leaf parsley, finely chopped

⅓ red (bell) pepper

2 teaspoons ground cumin

2 teaspoons ground coriander

1 teaspoon chilli/hot red pepper flakes

2 tablespoons plain/all-purpose flour

2 teaspoons baking powder

175 ml/¾ cup water

1 litre/quart vegetable oil, for deep frying

for the taratoor sauce

175 ml/¾ cup tahini

juice of 2 lemons

1 garlic clove, minced

175 ml/¾ cup water

1 teaspoon sea salt

handful of fresh flat-leaf parsley, finely chopped, plus extra to serve

8 pitta breads, toasted

a few leaves cos/romaine lettuce, to serve

2 tomatoes, sliced, to serve

fresh mint leaves, to garnish

sea salt and ground black pepper, to serve

4 gherkins/pickles, to serve

serves 4

Soak the chickpeas in a large bowl of cold water for at least 12 hours.

Drain the chickpeas and add to a food processor, along with the onion, salt, black pepper, garlic, bread, parsley, and red (bell) pepper, cumin and ground coriander. Blend until it reaches a granular consistency. Add the flour, 2 teaspoons of baking powder and the water and mix well.

Moisten your hands and form small balls of the chickpea mixture and flatten them slightly.

Heat the vegetable oil in a deep fryer or a large frying pan/skillet to 190°C (375°F) or until the oil is bubbling steadily. Fry the chickpea balls until golden brown. Remove the falafel and drain carefully using paper towels.

For the taratoor sauce, in a deep bowl, beat the tahini with the lemon juice and minced garlic until it becomes quite creamy. Add water little by little, and continue to beat well. Add the salt and parsley and stir. Taste and if the sauce isn't tangy enough, add a little bit more lemon juice. Refrigerate until ready to use.

To serve, stuff a couple of lettuce leaves into each pitta bread and add 2–3 falafel. Add the tomato slices, parsley, mint and salt and pepper. Drizzle on the sauce and serve with a gherkin/pickle.

Pad Thai is one of the most loved street foods in the world. Whether it be a rainy night take-out or ordered off a stall in an urban spot, it's easy to encounter various versions of this dish. If you prefer your pad Thai mild, remember to go easy on the fish sauce!

classic pad Thai

225 g/½ lb. banh pho rice noodles or flat white rice noodles,

12–16 king prawns/shrimp, peeled and deveined

1 teaspoon sugar

2 tablespoons fish sauce

2 tablespoons soy sauce

2 tablespoons tamarind paste, soaked in 2–3 tablespoons of warm water for 10 minutes

3 eggs

3 tablespoons vegetable oil

4 garlic cloves, sliced

60 g/½ cup firm tofu, cubed

30 g/½ cup bean sprouts

4 spring onions/scallions, green and white parts, roughly chopped

handful chopped coriander/cilantro, to serve

50 g/½ cup peanuts, crushed, to serve

1 lime, quartered, to serve

egg rolls (page 92), to serve

serves 4

You'll need to prepare all of the ingredients before you start cooking, as the stir fry process is quick! Soak the noodles in a pan of warm water for 20–25 minutes prior to cooking, drain and set aside. Peel the king prawns/shrimp and mix in a bowl with the sugar. Mix the fish sauce and soy sauce in a bowl. Strain the tamarind mixture and add it to soy and fish sauce mixture. In a separate bowl, beat the 3 eggs lightly and reserve.

Heat a wok on a medium-high heat. Add 2 tablespoons of vegetable oil and the garlic.

Stir fry for about 1 minute or just until the garlic browns. Add the prawns/shrimp and allow them to stir fry for about 2 minutes.

Add the tofu cubes and sear them for 1–2 minutes. Pour over the beaten egg and allow it to set for 2–3 minutes, then carefully break it up with a wooden spoon.

Remove the egg and king prawn/shrimp mixture from the wok and reserve.

Clean the wok and then heat it up again over a high heat. Add the remaining tablespoon of vegetable oil, and, when it's hot, add the drained noodles. Allow them to fry for about 1 minute. Add the tamarind and soy sauce mixture and stir. Add the bean sprouts and spring onions/scallions and stir the mixture for another 30 seconds. Add the king prawns/shrimp and tofu, cook for another couple of minutes and then serve immediately with coriander/cilantro, peanuts, and lime wedges.

Almost every big city in the US has a Mexican restaurant that boasts a "burrito as big as your head". In homage to this phenomenon, I've devised a tasty steak ranchero burrito recipe that's as big in size as it is in flavour.

steak ranchero burrito

4 large tortillas, to serve

1½ tablespoons olive oil

3 red (bell) peppers, sliced

2 medium onions, chopped

1½ tablespoons minced jalapeño peppers

4 garlic cloves, minced

1½ tablespoons dried thyme

1½ tablespoons dried oregano

4 fresh bay leaves

½ teaspoon chilli/hot red pepper flakes

500 ml/2 cups beef stock

200 g/1 cup fresh tomatoes, diced

skirt steak, about 900 g/2 lbs., cooked and cut into pieces

500 g/4 cups long-grain rice, cooked

90 g/1 cup Cheddar cheese, grated, to serve

sour cream, to serve

few sprigs coriander/cilantro, chopped, to serve

squeeze of lime juice

serves 4

Preheat an oven to 180°C (350°F) Gas 4. Wrap the tortillas in aluminium foil and place in the preheated oven for 15 minutes.

Meanwhile, heat the oil in a large frying pan/skillet over a medium heat. When the oil has heated up, add the vegetables, garlic, herbs and spices and sauté for 5 minutes. Add the beef stock and the diced tomatoes. Cook for another 4–5 minutes and add the steak and rice to the sauce for another 1–2 minutes.

Take the tortillas out of the oven carefully. Fill each one with the steak, rice and sauce mixture and fold to seal. Top with cheese, sour cream and a few sprigs of coriander/cilantro. Finish with a squeeze of lime juice.

SIDES

Because of its tangy, fresh taste, nothing goes with warm weather like homemade coleslaw. Along with hot dogs, cheeseburgers, BBQ baked beans and potato salad, it's a great component for a picnic or a get-together.

rosemary coleslaw

240 g/4 cups green or red cabbage, sliced or shredded thinly

1 large carrot, roughly grated

¼ medium red onion, chopped finely

1½ teaspoons sea salt, plus additional for seasoning

for the dressing

60 g/¼ cup mayonnaise

60 g/¼ cup sour cream

1 teaspoon Dijon mustard

60 ml/¼ cup cider vinegar

¼ teaspoon caraway seeds

¼ teaspoon ground black pepper

1 teaspoon fresh rosemary, chopped

1 teaspoon granulated sugar

1 small clove garlic, minced

pinch of cayenne pepper

serves 4

Place the cabbage, carrot and onion in a large colander set over a large bowl or plate, sprinkle with salt, and toss to coat. Place a heavy bowl on top of the cabbage, then place a heavy can or two in the bowl to weigh it down. Let it sit until the cabbage has released about 60 g/¼ cup of moisture, at least 1 hour.

Meanwhile, make the dressing. Add all the remaining ingredients, except the sugar, pepper and salt to a large sterilized jar, screw the lid on securely and shake. Add the sugar, pepper and salt to taste. Place the jar in the refrigerator for 30–60 minutes.

Transfer the cabbage, carrot and onion to a medium-size bowl and pour half the dressing over. Toss with tongs, cover and let the coleslaw sit for 30 minutes, tossing once or twice to redistribute the dressing. Toss once more before serving and add additional dressing if desired. Leftover dressing will keep for over 1 week in the refrigerator.

Although it might seem to some that fries should be prepared in a deep frier, I strongly suggest baking them in the oven. I find that cooking them in the oven delivers a better texture and crunch. It's also much easier to season them properly. These fries are crispy, golden and the perfect accompaniment to any sandwich. Eat them plain or dunk them in ketchup.

hand-cut fries

4 large baking potatoes

50 g/¼ cup olive oil

1 tablespoon paprika

1 tablespoon garlic pepper

1 tablespoon chilli powder

1 tablespoon onion powder

serves **4**

Preheat an oven to 180°C (350°F) Gas 4.

Use a sharp knife to cut the potatoes into 2.5 cm/1-in. thick wedges. In a medium-size mixing bowl, mix together the olive oil, paprika, garlic powder, chilli powder and onion powder. Coat the potatoes in this oil and spice mixture and place them on a baking sheet.

Bake the fries for 45 minutes to 1 hour in the preheated oven, turning once, and remove when they're golden and crispy.

If you're craving a high-fat and salty treat like French fries, try this delicious alternative instead. The crisp, caramelized edge conceals a soft and sweet centre. This recipe calls for olive oil, but coconut oil can be used instead if you like.

sweet potato fries

4 sweet potatoes cut to desired size and thickness

2–3 tablespoons olive oil

1 tablespoon salt

1 tablespoon ground black pepper

¼ teaspoon cayenne pepper (optional)

2 large baking sheets, greased liberally with olive oil

serves 4

Preheat an oven to 200°C (400°F) Gas 6.

Prepare the 2 baking sheets.

In a resealable plastic bag, combine the sweet potatoes, olive oil, salt, pepper and cayenne pepper. Close and shake the bag until the sweet potatoes are evenly coated. Spread them out in a single layer on the two baking sheets.

Bake in the preheated oven for 30 minutes, or until the sweet potatoes are crispy and brown on one side. Turn the fries over using a spatula, and cook for another 30 minutes, or until they are all crispy on the outside and tender inside.

Creamed corn is a recipe that most of us associate with an older generation, but like many classic recipes, it stays exciting with constant re-invention. **Mid-August** is the best time for this dish, as corn is at its peak then.

creamed corn & bacon

6 ears of fresh corn, removed from the cob

2 tablespoons olive oil

6 slices bacon, cooked and roughly chopped

4 tablespoons salted butter

2 tablespoons plain/all-purpose flour

(UK) 60 ml double cream and 60 ml whole milk, mixed, or (US) ½ cup half and half

2 tablespoons fresh coriander/cilantro, chopped, plus some to garnish

salt and pepper, to taste

serves 4–6

Remove the corn from the cobs and set aside.

Add 2 tablespoons of olive oil to a medium-size frying pan/skillet and add the bacon when the oil is hot. Turn the bacon slices after a couple of minutes and continue cooking until they've crisped up a bit. Place them on paper towels to soak up the grease. Allow them to cool before chopping, and set aside.

In a medium saucepan melt the remaining butter over a low heat. Whisk in the flour and then quickly whisk in the cream, a little at a time so that no clumps form. Stir in the bacon, corn, and coriander/cilantro. Taste and season with salt and pepper, as desired. Allow the mixture to simmer for a few minutes before removing from the heat.

Divide the corn mixture onto 4 serving plates and garnish with more coriander/cilantro.

Onion rings and French fries often compete for the title of main side dish. Although French fries are more common, it isn't until you have an onion ring in your mouth that you realize that if you were given the option, you would eat onion rings far more often. The batter used to coat the onions includes India pale ale (IPA) which adds a lovely richness. The alcohol cooks off when the onions are fried.

ale-battered onion rings

120 g/1 cup plain/all-purpose flour, plus extra for dusting

250 ml/1 cup India pale ale

2 large brown or Vidalia onions

canola oil, for frying

salt, to taste

yellow mustard, to serve

Homemade Ranch Dressing (page 56), to serve

serves 4

Put the flour into a mixing bowl and make a well in the centre. Pour the ale into the well and whisk until combined. Let the mixture rest, covered for 1 hour.

Peel the onions and cut crosswise into 1-cm/^{1}/3-in.thick rings. Dust the rings with more flour, shaking off the excess, and coat them with the batter.

Heat 5 cm/2 in. of canola oil in a large frying pan/skillet. The pan is at the right temperature when the oil is steadily bubbling. Working in batches, fry the onion rings until they're golden in colour. Use a slotted spoon to transfer the onion rings onto paper towels to drain. Sprinkle them with salt to taste.

Dip them in ranch dressing and yellow mustard.

Maple Baked Beans are a great side
dish, particularly during the cooler months.
This recipe uses pure maple syrup, ketchup and BBQ sauce
to produce a tangy and sweet flavour.

maple baked beans

8 slices fried bacon, chopped into pieces

450 g/1 lb. dry haricot/navy beans

5 litres/quarts cold water

1 onion, chopped

200 g/^{2}/$_3$ cup pure maple syrup

90 ml/^{1}/$_3$ cup tomato ketchup

60 ml/^{1}/$_4$ cup BBQ sauce (page 64)

5 teaspoons cider vinegar

1 teaspoon prepared mustard

1 teaspoon sea salt

^{1}/$_2$ teaspoon ground black pepper

serves 4

Fry the bacon in a frying pan/skillet and chop roughly into pieces. Set aside.

Rinse the beans and place them in a pan with a tight-fitting lid. Add 3 litres/quarts of cold water. Bring to a boil and reduce heat. Simmer for 2 minutes.

Remove from heat, cover and let stand for 1 hour.

Drain and rinse the beans. Return the beans to the pan and add the remaining water. Bring the mixture to a boil over a medium to high heat, reduce the heat to low-medium and let simmer for about 40 minutes, or until almost tender. Drain and reserve the liquid.

Preheat an oven to 150°C (300°F) Gas 2.

In a large bowl, combine the beans and all the remaining ingredients. Pour the mixture into a large casserole dish. Cover and bake in the preheated oven at 150°C (300°F) Gas 2 for 2^1/$_2$ hours, or until tender. Stir the beans occasionally and add a little of the reserved bean water if too much juice has evaporated during cooking.

Fried green tomatoes are popular in the southern part of the US. This recipe is simple to prepare – frying unripened tomatoes in vegetable oil after coating them with a mixture of flour, cornmeal and a little salt and pepper. Panko breadcrumbs are ideal for this recipe and are available from large supermarkets or Asian food stores.

fried green tomatoes

4 large green tomatoes

2 eggs

125 ml/½ cup milk

120 g/1 cup plain/
all-purpose flour

65 g/½ cup cornmeal

60 g/½ cup panko or
ordinary breadcrumbs

2 teaspoons coarse sea salt

¼ teaspoon ground black
pepper

vegetable oil, for frying

serves 4

Chop the tomatoes into 1.25-cm/½-in. thick slices, discarding the ends. You should have 4–5 pieces per tomato. Set aside on a large plate.

In a medium bowl, whisk the eggs and milk together.

Measure out the flour and put it on a plate. In a separate bowl, whisk together the cornmeal, breadcrumbs, salt and pepper and transfer the mixture to a plate.

First, dip the tomato slices into the flour to coat, then dip them into the milk and egg mixture. Finally, dip them into the breadcrumb mixture so that they are completely covered in them.

Pour vegetable oil to a depth of 1.25 cm/½ in. into a large frying pan/skillet and heat over a medium heat. When the oil is steadily bubbling, carefully place the tomatoes into the frying pan/skillet in batches of 4 or 5, depending on the size of your frying pan/skillet. Do not crowd the tomatoes – they should not touch each other. When the tomatoes are browned, flip and fry them on the other side. Drain them on paper towels.

Pickles are a staple around the globe, from Europe to the southern regions of the US – where, the dill pickle is fried or soaked along with the flavoured drink mix Kool-Aid for a sweet & sour treat. Kool-Aid can be found in some large UK supermarkets and online. These three pickles will keep for two weeks in the refrigerator.

spicy dill pickles

1 litre/4 cups water

300 ml/1¼ cups white vinegar

3 tablespoons sea salt

8 dill sprigs

8 large cloves garlic

4 dried hot chilli/chile peppers

675 g/24 oz. pickling cucumbers, quartered or halved and sliced lengthwise

4 x sterilized 450 ml/16 oz. canning jars

makes 4 jars

In a stainless steel stockpot, bring the water, vinegar and salt to a boil. Let boil for 10–12 minutes.

Meanwhile, pack the cucumbers facing upwards into canning jars. Make sure they are at least 1.25 cm/½ in. below the jar's rim. Place 2 dill sprigs, 2 garlic cloves and 1 chilli/chile pepper in each jar. Carefully ladle the hot mixture into the jars. Add extra water if necessary so that the cucumbers are submerged, but leave 1.25 cm/½ in. of space from the rim of the jar. Remove air bubbles, wipe the rims and put the lids on. Let the cucumbers pickle for at least 24 hours before tasting.

sweet pickles

240 ml/1 cup cider vinegar

40 g/⅛ cup salt

200 g/1 cup granulated sugar

¼ teaspoon ground turmeric

½ teaspoon mustard seed

400 g/14 oz. pickling cucumbers, quartered or halved and sliced lengthwise

1 sweet onion, sliced

2 x sterilized 450 ml/16 oz. canning jars

makes 2 jars

In a small saucepan over a medium-high heat, combine the cider vinegar, salt, sugar, turmeric and mustard seed. Bring to a boil and let cook for 5 minutes.

Loosely pack the cucumbers and the onion into canning jars and pour the hot liquid over them. Remove air bubbles, wipe the rims and put the lids on. Let the cucumbers pickle for at least 24 hours before tasting.

sweet & sour cherry pickles

½ jar spicy dill pickles (see left), including the brine

1 packet cherry Kool-Aid powder

200 g/1 cup granulated sugar

1 x sterilized 450 ml/16 oz. canning jar

makes 1 jar

Follow the recipe to the left for spicy dill pickles.

After the brining is done, remove the pickles from the liquid. Stir in the sugar and the Kool-Aid to the pickle brine until they have both dissolved. Add the pickles back to the mixture, and seal in the jar. Place in the refrigerator and let brine for at least 1 week before tasting.

TREATS

This pie is something everyone should try once. For the best result use a mixture of apples – I like to bake it with two Gala, two Jonagold and one Honeycrisp. The lattice crust is attractive, but not essential to the flavour!

apple cheddar pie

for the Cheddar pie crust

400 g/3 cups all-purpose flour

1/2 teaspoon salt

225 g/2 sticks unsalted butter, cut into small pieces and chilled

225 g/8 oz. mature/sharp cheddar, grated/shredded

60 ml/1/4 cup ice water

60 ml/1/4 cup white vinegar

for the salted caramel sauce

200 g/1 cup white sugar

80 ml/1/4 cup water

115 g/1 stick unsalted butter

120 ml/1/2 cup double/heavy cream

1 1/2 teaspoons fine sea salt

for the filling

freshly squeezed juice of 1 lemon

5–6 medium to large apples

65 g/1/3 cup golden/raw sugar

2 tablespoons plain/all-purpose flour

1/4 teaspoon ground cinnamon

1/4 teaspoon ground allspice

for the streusel topping

150 g/3/4 cup granulated sugar

100 g/3/4 cup plain/all-purpose flour

1 tablespoon ice-cold water

1 1/2 teaspoons ground cinnamon

70 g/1/2 stick butter, softened

serves 8

To make the pie crust, combine the flour and salt in a large bowl. Work in the butter pieces with your hands until the mixture is in pea-size crumbs. Stir in the cheese. Combine the water and vinegar and gradually stir it in until the mixture forms a ball. Divide the dough in half and shape into balls. Wrap in clingfilm/plastic wrap and refrigerate for 4 hours or overnight. Roll one ball out to fit a 23-cm/9-in. pie plate. Place the bottom crust in the pie plate. Roll out the top crust on a piece of baking parchment and transfer both crusts to the refrigerator until needed.

To make the salted caramel, gently heat the sugar and water together in a small saucepan set over low heat until just dissolved. Add the butter and bring to a slow boil. Continue cooking at a low boil until the mixture turns a deep, golden brown. This process may take up to an hour so have patience! Once the mixture is ready, remove it from the heat and immediately add the cream – it will bubble rapidly and steam – take care as it will be very hot. Whisk the resulting mixture together over a low heat and sprinkle in the sea salt. Set the caramel aside until needed.

To make the apple pie filling, put the lemon juice in a large mixing bowl. Core, peel, and thinly slice the whole apples into 2.5-cm/1-in. slices.

Toss the apple slices into the lemon juice as you cut them to prevent them from browning. Set the prepared apples aside.

In a small mixing bowl, combine the sugar, flour, cinnamon, and allspice. Whisk to combine. Sprinkle this mixture over the apples and use your hands to gently toss and coat the apple slices.

Preheat the oven to 190°C (375°F) Gas 5.

Gather your rolled pie crust, salted caramel and apple mixture. Begin by layering one third of the apples in the bottom of the crust so that there are minimal gaps. Pour one third of the caramel lightly over the apples. Add one third of the apples and caramel for a second layer, and then add a third layer of apples, and then the caramel again.

Assemble the lattice crust (if doing) and flute the edges of the crust. Brush the crust with a beaten egg and lightly sprinkle with 1 tablespoon of raw sugar and sea salt.

Put the pie on a large baking sheet and bake in the preheated oven for 20 minutes. Reduce the oven temperature to 175°C (350°F) Gas 4 and bake for a further 25–35 minutes. You can test the apples for doneness with a skewer – they should should be just soft.

Let the pie cool for at least 30 minutes while you make a streusel topping. Mix all the ingredients until crumbly and spread on a baking sheet. Bake for 15–20 minutes in an oven preheated to 175°C (350°F) Gas 4 until golden. Let cool briefly and then use to top the apple pie.

Cherry pie is one of the world's most beloved treats and staple of any good, red-blooded diner. It's best served with ice cream or, à la mode.

diner-style cherry pie

for the fuss-free pie crust

340 g/2½ cups plain/all-purpose flour, plus extra for rolling

1 teaspoon fine sea salt

230 g/2 sticks cold unsalted butter, cut into small pieces

60–120 ml/¼–½ cup iced water

1 egg beaten with 2 tablespoons water or milk to make a 'wash'

1 tablespoon caster/granulated sugar, for sprinkling

for the filling

600 g/4 cups fresh sweet cherries, such as Merchant or Bing, pitted (if you don't have a pitter, use a pastry or cake decorating nozzle/tip to push the pits out)

200–300 g/ 1–1½ cups granulated sugar

4 tablespoons cornflour/cornstarch

½ tablespoon almond extract

a 23-cm/9-in. shallow pie dish/plate, greased

a baking sheet lined with parchment paper

serves 8

In a food processor, combine the flour, salt and sugar and pulse briefly. Add the butter and pulse until the mixture resembles coarse meal, with a few pea-size pieces of butter remaining. Sprinkle with 60 ml/¼ cup iced water. Pulse until the dough is crumbly but holds together when squeezed. If necessary, add up to 60 ml/¼ cup more water but a little at a time. Divide the dough into 2 pieces, one just slightly larger than the other. Shape each one into a 2-cm/1-in. thick disk and wrap in clingfilm/plastic wrap. Chill for at least 1 hour.

When ready, take the dough out of the refrigerator and let it come to room temperature. Lightly flour a work surface and a rolling pin. Roll the larger one out to a 33–35 cm/13–14 in. round and the smaller one to a 30.5 cm/12 in. round, periodically turning them and sprinkling flour as necessary. Fold the larger one into quarters and transfer to the pie dish/plate. Then, gently unfold the dough and ease it up the sides of the dish. Let the dough overhang by about 2 cm/1 in. and trim the excess away with a paring knife. Place the smaller one on the prepared baking sheet. Refrigerate both for 15 minutes, while you make the filling.

Put the cherries in a large saucepan, place over a low heat and cover. After the cherries leak considerable juice, which may take a few minutes, mix the sugar and cornflour/cornstarch together, tip into the hot cherries and mix well. Continue cooking over a low heat until the juice is thickened and translucent Remove from the heat, stir in the almond extract, and let cool completely.

Preheat the oven to 190°C (375°F) Gas 5. Remove the dough from the fridge. Moisten the rim of the pie shell with egg wash. Spoon the cooled cherry filling into the pie. Cover the filling with the top crust and press the edges together with your fingers or the tines of a fork to seal. Brush the top crust with the rest of the egg wash and sprinkle with sugar. Using a paring knife, create a steam vent by cutting slits in the dough to form the shape of star. Bake the pie in the preheated oven for 50 minutes, until the crust is golden.

Transfer the pie to a wire rack to cool. The pie is best served 2–3 hours after it is baked, but it can be kept at room temperature the day it is baked or wrapped and refrigerated for up to 3 days.

*So simple but oh so delicious!
Serve a scoop with a slice of warm
apple pie or brownie or on its own,
drizzled with extra honey. Yum.*

honey vanilla ice cream

500 ml/2 cups double/
heavy cream

500 ml/2 cups whole milk

85 g/¼ cup runny honey

1 teaspoon vanilla extract or
vanilla bean paste

10 very fresh egg yolks
(UK medium/US large)

6 tablespoons granulated sugar

a pinch of fine sea salt

a prepared ice bath

an ice cream maker

makes 1 litre/1 quart

Combine the cream, milk, honey and vanilla extract
in a large saucepan and set over a medium heat,
stirring to dissolve the honey.

As the cream mixture warms, whisk together the
egg yolks, sugar and salt in a mixing bowl.

When the cream mixture is hot and the honey
has melted, temper the eggs by slowly pouring a
few ladlefuls or tablespoons of the hot mixture
into the eggs, whisking the eggs constantly to
prevent the eggs from cooking.

Pour the tempered egg mixture into the saucepan
and cook over low heat, stirring until the mixture
has thickened enough to stick to the spoon and
not run, if you wipe your finger along the spoon
covered with custard.

Strain the custard through a sieve/strainer into a
clean bowl and place in the prepared ice bath,
stirring occasionally to cool. Cover the ice cream
and refrigerate for several hours, until it is cold.

Transfer the mixture to an ice cream maker and
churn according to the manufacturer's
instructions.

Serve immediately for soft serve or freeze and
use within a few days.

The flavour of salted caramel seems to have come from nowhere to be one of the most celebrated treats from popcorn to fine chocolate. This recipe won't disappoint die-hard fans and will definitely seduce the uninitiated! Serve with a warm brownie or just as it comes.

salted caramel ice cream

120 ml/½ cup water

430 g/2 cups granulated sugar plus 2 tablespoons

1 tablespoon vanilla extract

2½ teaspoons Fleur de Sel (pure, unrefined French sea salt)

420 ml/1¾ cups double/ heavy cream

1 litre/4 cups whole milk

9 very fresh egg yolks (UK medium/US large

sugar/candy thermometer

a prepared ice bath

an ice cream maker

makes 1 litre/quart

To make the salted caramel. Combine the water and 400 g/2 cups of the sugar in a small heavy-bottomed saucepan. Heat the mixture over a low heat, stirring occasionally until the sugar is completely dissolved. Raise the heat to medium and cook without stirring until the syrup turns a rich caramel colour. Stir the vanilla extract and Fleur de Sel into the caramel and set aside until needed.

Heat the cream in a large saucepan. Once simmering, spoon a little of the cream into the caramel. Return all of the caramel-cream mixture to the pan, add the milk and bring to the boil.

Meanwhile, whisk the egg yolks and remaining sugar together in a large bowl. Once the milk scalds, take it off the heat and add some of the caramel-milk into the eggs, about 60 ml/¼ cup at a time so that you don't cook the eggs. Add the egg and milk mixture to the pan, return to the hob/stove and cook until a sugar/candy thermometer reads 76°C (170°F) or until the mixture coats the back of a spoon.

Strain the custard through a sieve/strainer into a clean bowl and place in the prepared ice bath, stirring occasionally to cool. Cover the mixture and refrigerate for several hours, until it is cold.

Transfer the mixture into an ice cream maker and churn according to the manufacturer's instructions.

Serve immediately for soft serve or freeze and use within a few days.

There is nothing like a good chocolate cake. Let's face it, chocolate is one of the highways to a woman's soul and this cake is no exception. It's density is light, decadent and when paired here with chocolate meringue buttercream frosting, it's absolutely sublime.

decadent chocolate cake
with meringue buttercream

30 g/¼ cup unsweetened cocoa powder

45 g/⅓ cup plain/all-purpose flour

⅛ teaspoon baking powder

a pinch of fine sea salt

60 g/½ stick butter, softened

100 g/½ cup granulated sugar

2 eggs

3 tablespoons buttermilk

½ teaspoon vanilla extract or vanilla bean paste

for the meringue buttercream

170 g/¾ cup plus 1 heaping tablespoon white sugar

120 ml/½ cup egg whites (Note: this frosting contains raw egg and is not suitable for pregnant women)

425 g/4 sticks unsalted butter, at room temperature and cut into 5-cm/2-in. cubes

140 g/5 oz good-quality dark/semisweet chocolate

1½ teaspoons vanilla extract or vanilla bean paste

a 20-cm/8-in. square baking pan, greased and floured

a sugar/candy thermometer

a stand mixer

serves 8–10

Preheat the oven to 175°C (350°F) Gas 4.

Sift the cocoa powder, plain/all-purpose flour, baking powder and salt into a mixing bowl. Set aside until needed.

Cream together the butter and sugar in a mixing bowl. Combine the buttermilk and vanilla in a small bowl or measuring jug/cup. Alternate adding the buttermilk and the cocoa powder-flour mixture to the butter-sugar mixture. Starting with the buttermilk, add 1 tablespoon of the buttermilk to the butter mixture, mix until just combined and then add one third of the cocoa powder/flour mixture. Repeat until combined, scraping the sides of the bowl after each addition. Pour into the prepared baking pan and bake in the preheated oven for 15–25 minutes, or until a skewer inserted in the middle of the cake comes out clean. Remove the cake from the oven and leave to cool on a wire rack.

To make the meringue buttercream, put the sugar and 3 tablespoons cold water in a small heavy-bottomed saucepan and bring to the boil. Use a sugar/candy thermometer to monitor the temperature of the mixture. The goal is to bring the mixture to 115°C (240°F).

While the water and sugar are boiling, put the egg whites in the bowl of a stand mixer and beat on medium-high until softly peaking, then slowly beat in the sugar until the mixture is stiffly peaking.

Once the sugar-water mixture has boiled and reached the desired temperature, adjust the stand mixer speed to medium and slowly beat in the hot syrup. Pour the sugar/water in so that is trickles slowly into the egg whites. If the hot sugar mixture is poured too fast it will cook the egg. After the addition of the sugar-water mixture, beat the mixture for about 8–10 minutes until the mixture is cool and you have stiff, glossy peaks. Beat in the butter, a cube at a time until the mixture is thickened and smooth.

Melt the chocolate with the vanilla in a heatproof bowl set over a pan of barely simmering water. Pouring half at a time, add to the buttercream and fold in. Use a palette knife to spread the buttercream over the cooled chocolate cake. Refrigerate until ready to enjoy.

This recipe was inspired by a French Silk Pie. However, I found that a Gianduja pastry cream far surpassed a Gianduja mousse. This pie meshes hazelnut and chocolate with almond cookie crust and lightly sweetened whipped cream. It's an absolute must if you love almonds!

Gianduja chocolate cream pie

for the almond pie crust

24 Almond Cookies (see page 143) or store-bought almond biscuits/cookies, as preferred

1 tablespoon granulated sugar

1 teaspoon salt

60 g/½ stick unsalted butter, melted

for the filling

500 ml/2 cups Luxury Chocolate Pudding (see page 140)

500 ml/2 cups double/ heavy cream

1 tablespoon white sugar

1 teaspoon vanilla extract or vanilla bean paste

dark/bittersweet chocolate, for grating

a 23-cm/9-in. flan/pie plate, greased

serves 8–10

To make the almond pie crust, preheat an oven to 175°C (350°F) Gas 4.

Put the almond cookies in a resealable plastic bag. Seal it and bash the cookies with a rolling pin to crush them into crumbs. You will need about 200 g/2 cups of crumbs. Tip them into a mixing bowl and add the sugar and salt. Add the melted butter and mix to blend.

Use your fingers to press the crumb mixture onto the bottom and up sides of the prepared flan/pie dish.

Bake in the preheated oven for about 10 minutes, until golden around edges. Leave to cool completely in the dish on a wire cooling rack. Using either a stand mixer or hand-held whisk, whip the cream and sugar together until medium peaks form. If you overmix, just add more cream. Beat in the vanilla extract.

Fill the cooled almond cookie crust with the Luxury Chocolate Pudding. Spread the whipped cream over the top and grate chocolate over the pie to finish. Refrigerate until ready to serve.

Technically this recipe is more of a pastry cream than a pudding but it fits the bill perfectly. You can use it as a pie filling (page 136), serve it simply with whipped cream, fill cupcakes or even freeze it for popsicles! This recipes uses hazelnut Gianduja but any good dark chocolate will work.

luxury chocolate pudding

500 ml/2 cups whole milk

500 ml/2 cups double/heavy cream

1 very fresh egg plus 2 yolks (UK medium, US large)

200 g/1 cup granulated sugar

30 g/¼ cup plus 1 teaspoon cornflour/cornstarch

3 heaping tablespoons unsweetened cocoa powder

40 g/3 tablespoons unsalted butter, softened

60 g/2 oz. Gianduja hazelnut chocolate (or any good 72% chocolate), melted

½ teaspoon vanilla extract

serves 6–8

Put the milk and cream in a large saucepan set over a low heat and bring the mixture to a medium simmer.

In a large, heat-resistant bowl, whisk together the eggs, egg yolks, sugar, cornflour/cornstarch and cocoa powder. When the milk comes to a boil, slowly temper it into the egg mixture 2–3 tablespoons at a time. Do not pour the milk in at once, it will cook the eggs and you will have chocolate scrambled eggs!

Return the mixture to the saucepan and bring it back to the heat. Cook over low-medium heat until the mixture is thick and glossy.

Remove the pan from heat and add the butter, melted chocolate and vanilla extract. Strain through a sieve/strainer to remove chunks or cooked egg. Serve warm or store in the refrigerator with a layer of clingfilm/plastic wrap covering the surface of the pudding.

Almond cookies are not only a tasty tea-time treat or a wonderful ending to an Asian-inspired meal, but they also make a delicious pie crust.

almond cookies

115 g/1 stick unsalted butter, softened

100 g/½ cup granulated sugar

1 egg, lightly beaten

2 teaspoons almond extract or Amaretto di Saronno almond-flavoured liqueur

50 g/½ cup ground almonds

160 g/1¼ cups plain/ all-purpose flour, sifted

1—2 baking sheets, lined with baking parchment

makes 24

Preheat oven to 200°C (400°F) Gas 6.

In a large bowl, cream together the butter and sugar. Beat in the egg, almond extract and almonds. Gradually mix in the flour until well blended.

Use a teaspoon to gently drop about 48 small blobs of the mixture spaced 5 cm/2 in. apart on the prepared baking sheets.

Bake in the preheated oven for 5–8 minutes, until the cookies are lightly coloured. Remove from the oven, leave to cool for about 10 minutes on the baking sheets and then carefully transfer to a wire rack to cool completely.

The cookies will keep for up to 5 days if stored in an airtight container.

Estate chocolate is becoming a big trend around the world. Bean-to-bar cocoa is popping up on dessert menus from Paris to New York. Valrhona's Ampamakia is a representative of cacao grown in Madagascar. The aroma and taste of the bar is earthy with a hint of strawberry, vanilla and tangerine mixed with a buttery-vanilla flavour and takes the humble brownie to new heights of gourmet indulgence!

estate chocolate brownies

100 g/³⁄₄ cup plain/all-purpose flour, sifted

75 g/³⁄₄ cup unsweetened alkalized cocoa powder such as the Swizz brand Felchlin (if using regular cocoa powder, use 100 g/1 cup)

1 teaspoon fine sea salt

345 g/3 sticks unsalted butter, cut into cubes

3 large eggs

350 g/1³⁄₄ cups granulated sugar

¹⁄₂ teaspoon pure vanilla extract or vanilla bean paste

200 g/7 oz. Valrhona Ampamakia (64% or 70% according to your own taste) or other dark/bittersweet chocolate, chopped

icing/confectioners' sugar or powdered sugar for dusting (optional)

a 23-cm/9-in. square brownie pan, greased and floured

makes 12

Preheat the oven to 175°C (350°F) Gas 4.

Sift the flour, cocoa powder and salt into a mixing bowl and set aside until needed.

Put half the butter cubes in a medium heatproof bowl and set aside.

Put the remaining butter cubes in a saucepan set over a medium heat and melt, stirring. Pour the melted butter over the cubed butter and stir to combine. The butter should look creamy, with bits of unmelted butter still present and floating.

Put the eggs, sugar and vanilla extract in a separate bowl and beat with a handheld electric whisk set to a medium speed for about 3 minutes, until the mixture is light and doubled in volume.

Using a lower speed, alternate adding the flour and the butter in several additions. Stir in 175 g/6 oz. of the chopped chocolate, reserving the rest.

Pour the mixture into the prepared pan and scatter the reserved pieces of chocolate over the top. Bake in the preheated oven for 35–40 minutes, until the surface looks firm but a skewer inserted in the centre comes out slightly sticky with mixture.

Let the brownie cool in the pan before cutting into 12 squares. Dust lightly with icing/confectioner's sugar (if using) just before serving.

This is really good topped with a scoop of Salted Caramel Ice Cream (see page 135).

Rice pudding is not often a first choice for dessert but it can be found (if you're lucky), in a rotating display case in neighbourhood American diners. Traditionally, rice pudding contains raisins, and in this pimped up version, the sweetness of the raisins is enhanced with salted caramel and pistachios, adding crunch and texture. Give it a go!

rice pudding
with salted caramel sauce

1 litre/4 cups whole milk

140 g/²/₃ cup uncooked short grain white rice

a pinch of salt

2 eggs

50 g/¼ cup dark muscovado sugar

1 teaspoon vanilla extract

¼ teaspoon ground cinnamon

for the salted caramel sauce

200 g/1 cup granulated white sugar

125 ml/½ cup water

175 ml/³/₄ cup double/ heavy cream

1 teaspoon sea salt or Fleur de Sel (pure, unrefined French sea salt)

a handful of raisins, sultanas and/or crushed pistachios, to garnish (optional)

serves 4

Put the milk, rice and pinch of salt in a medium-sized, heavy-bottomed saucepan and set over a high heat. Bring to the boil then reduce the heat to low and simmer for 20–25 minutes, until the rice is tender. Stir frequently with a wooden spoon to prevent the rice from sticking to the bottom of the pan.

In a small mixing bowl, whisk together the egg and brown sugar until well mixed. Add 125 ml/½ cup of the hot rice mixture to the egg mixture, a tablespoon at a time, vigorously whisking to incorporate.

Return the egg mixture to the saucepan of rice and milk and cook, on low heat, for 5–10 minutes, stirring continuously until thickened. Be careful not to let the mixture come to the boil at this point or it will curdle. Remove from the heat and stir in the vanilla extract and cinnamon. Spoon the pudding into a serving dish and chill in the refrigerator until ready to serve.

To make the salted caramel sauce, combine the sugar and 60 ml/¼ cup of the water in a small saucepan. Heat the mixture over a low heat, stirring occasionally until the sugar is completely dissolved. Increase the heat to medium and cook without stirring until the syrup turns a rich caramel colour. Remove the pan from the heat add the remaining water and the cream and salt. It will be very hot and may splatter so take care. Transfer to a small jug/pitcher and set aside to cool completely.

When ready to serve, take the rice pudding out of the refrigerator. Scatter over the raisins, sultanas and pistachios (if using). Serve with the salted caramel sauce on the side so more or less can be added to taste, as it is very rich and sweet.

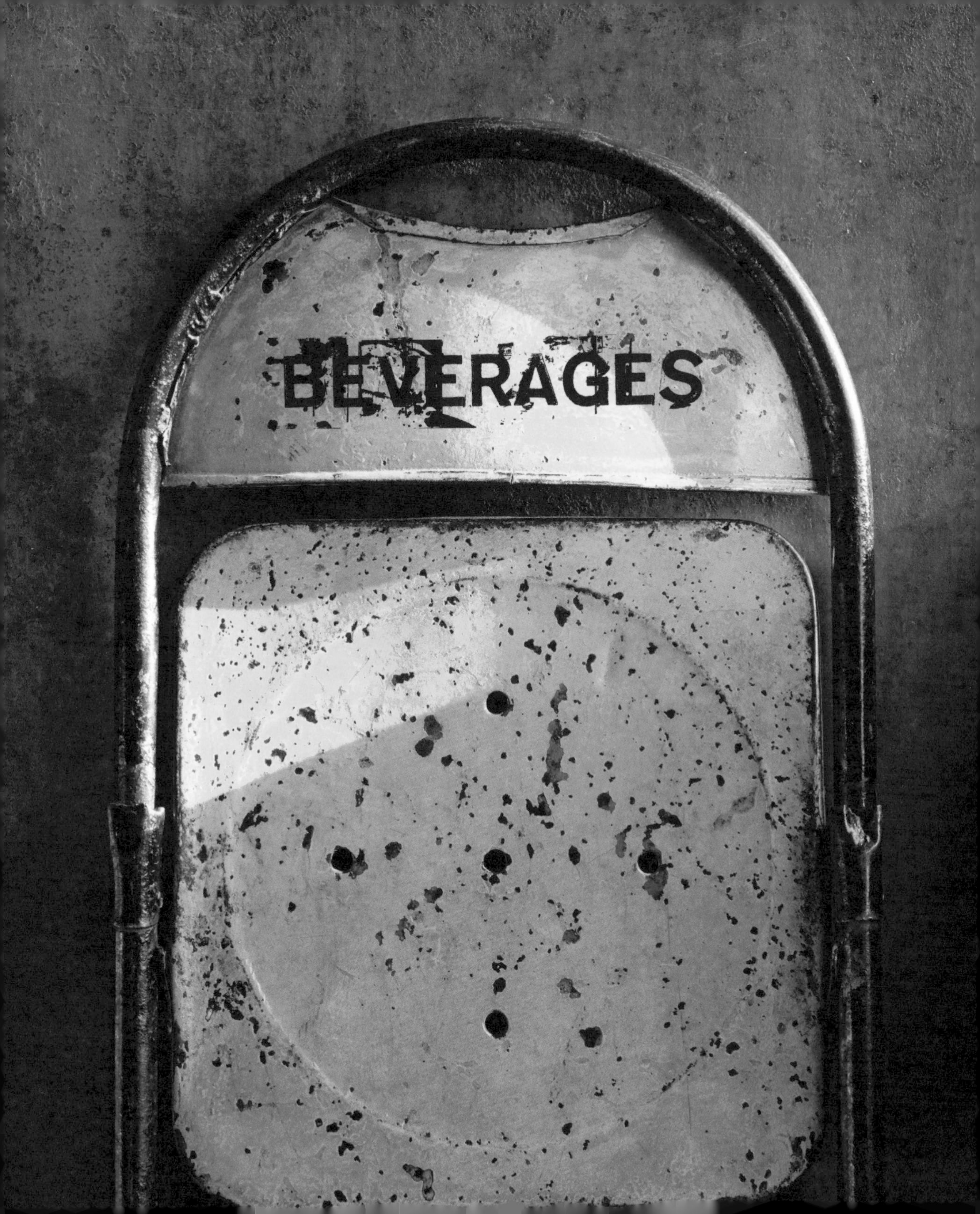
BEVERAGES

A kids' drink that's all grown up, this is the kind of peculiar recipe that people love or hate!

honey-vanilla root beer float

500 ml/2 cups water

4 tablespoons sassafras extract

1 tablespoon honey

60–100 g/$\frac{1}{3}$–$\frac{1}{2}$ cup brown sugar

5 cloves

12 peppercorns

5-cm/2-in. piece of ginger, peeled and chopped

a few mint leaves

carbonated/soda water, to serve

Honey Vanilla Ice Cream (page 132), to serve

serves about 4

Combine all the ingredients in a saucepan and simmer over a medium heat for about 15 minutes. Remove from the heat, cover and allow to steep for about 30 minutes.

Allow the syrup to cool completely before straining through a sieve/strainer to get rid of the solids. Pour the syrup into a little bottle. It will store in the fridge for a few days.

To serve, combine about 4 tablespoons of the syrup with carbonated/soda water in a tall glass and stir. Add 2 small scoops of Honey Vanilla Ice Cream to each glass.

There are so many different ways of making Thai tea, but I love the richness the cardamom, cloves and cinnamon add to this variation. Serve cold over ice.

Thai iced-tea

1.45 litres/6 cups water

60 g/1 cup Thai or black tea leaves

4 cardamom pods, crushed

1 whole clove, crushed

¼ teaspoon cinnamon

200 g/1 cup granulated sugar

(UK) 120 ml double cream and 120 ml whole milk, mixed or (US) 1 cup half and half

crushed ice, to serve

makes 1.7 litres/1⁴/₅ quarts

In a medium saucepan, bring the water to the boil.

Stir in the tea leaves and crushed cardamom pods, crushed clove and cinnamon.

Cover and remove the mixture from heat and let steep 5 minutes.

Pour the brewed tea through a fine wire-mesh sieve/strainer into a jug/pitcher (not a glass one, as it may break), discarding the tea leaves. Add the sugar, and stir until it has dissolved; cool. Cover and chill for 2 hours.

Serve in glasses over crushed ice.

Top with a couple of tablespoons of the cream mixture/half and half and it's ready to drink!

We're experiencing an age of powdered drink mixes, frozen food and dried fruit, but sometimes it's nice to go back to basics, such as with this classic American staple.

homemade lemonade

350 g/1³/₄ cups granulated sugar

2 litres/2 quarts water

375 ml/1¹/₂ cups freshly squeezed lemon juice

makes 2.6 litres/2⁴/₅ quarts

In a small saucepan, combine the sugar and 250 ml/1 cup water. Bring to the boil and stir to dissolve the sugar. Allow to cool to room temperature, then cover and refrigerate until chilled.

Remove the seeds from the lemon juice, but leave the pulp. Fetch a large jug/pitcher and stir together the chilled syrup, the lemon juice and remaining water. Your thirst-quenching lemonade is now ready!

This adults-only milkshake combines the best of both worlds – milkshake and bourbon. Add whipped cream, nuts and a cherry to really shake it up.

salted caramel bourbon milkshake

1 litre/4 cups Salted Caramel Ice Cream (page 145)

250 ml/1 cup chocolate milk

1 teaspoon sea salt

150 ml/^{2}/$_3$ cup bourbon

ice, cubed (optional)

serves 4

Blend the ice cream, chocolate milk, sea salt and bourbon in a blender, adding ice depending how thick you want your shake. Pour into lowball glasses or tumblers.

This frosty treat is summertime's answer to hot chocolate. Adding ice and whipped cream to a hot chocolate recipe creates the perfect combination of ice cream and shake.

cold drinking chocolate

60 g/^{1}/$_3$ cup and 1 tablespoon sifted icing/confectioners' sugar

2 tablespoons and 1^1/$_2$ teaspoons unsweetened cocoa powder

2 tablespoons and 2 teaspoons powdered non-dairy creamer/coffee whitener

500 ml/ 2 cups whole milk

1 litre/4 cups ice

250 ml/1 cup double/heavy cream, whipped

2 tablespoons granulated sugar

40 g/^{1}/$_4$ cup mini chocolate chips or grated chocolate

serves 4

Whisk together the icing/confectioners' sugar, cocoa powder and creamer/coffee whitener.

Place the milk into a blender and add the dry chocolate mixture. Blend until the ingredients have combined. Add ice and blend until the ice is in tiny chunks. Pour the mixture evenly into 4 glasses on top of separate plates (to catch any dripping frozen hot chocolate).

Top each glass with whipped cream and sprinkle with mini chocolate chips.

The margarita is essential for any Mexican fiesta, and this version celebrates the world-famous drink in its truest form.

margarita

salt, for the glass rim (optional)

ice cubes

180 ml/³/₄ cup tequila (I recommend Patron Silver)

120 ml/¹/₂ cup freshly squeezed lime juice

1 tablespoon freshly squeezed orange juice

3 tablespoons Cointreau

makes 350 ml/1½ cups

If using salt, place a couple of teaspoons in a shallow dish. Moisten the rim of a lowball glass or a tumbler with a dampened paper towel, then dip the top of the glass in salt.

Fill the glass with ice, then add the tequila, lime juice, orange juice and Cointreau; stir a few times, then serve immediately.

This rich, luxurious version of a classic cream soda strikes the perfect balance between bitter and sweet. Substitute the stout for soda/carbonated water for a delicious non-alcoholic version.

stout cream soda

400 g/2 cups brown sugar

500 ml/2 cups water

freshly squeezed juice of 1 lemon

1 teaspoon vanilla paste or 1 vanilla bean/pod split, with the seeds set aside

ice cubes, for serving

330 ml/11 fl. oz. can stout or 330 ml/11 fl. oz soda/carbonated water, for serving

makes 500 ml/2 cups

Place the sugar and 60 ml/¹/₄ cup water in a medium-size non-reactive saucepan. Heat over a medium-high heat until the sugar has caramelized.

Carefully add the rest of the water and the lemon juice, then add the vanilla paste or vanilla bean/pod and the reserved seeds and bring to a boil. Remove from heat and let stand for 1 hour.

Discard the vanilla bean/pod and transfer the syrup to an airtight container. This syrup may be kept, refrigerated, for up to 2 weeks.

To serve, fill a 500 ml/16 fl. oz glass with ice cubes and add 3 tablespoons of the syrup. Slowly pour the stout or carbonated/soda water into the glass and stir to combine.

INDEX

acknowledgements

First and foremost, I would like to thank my hometown, Chicago. Chicago, you are a city that inspires me — your food, your drinks, your weather, your people. My people. I love you. Next, I would also like to thank my friends: Ashley Arteaga, Steve and Patrice Yursik, Jill T. Glass, Megan Lalleman, Anthony Rubinas, Hillary Welsh, and Ian & the Tomeles (it should be a band name). I would also like to thank the wonderful people at Green Zebra restaurant in Chicago, who, while I worked on a cookbook by day with a miserable attitude after breaking my foot in the middle of summer, helped me at night at my day job, making me laugh and teaching me quite a bit about food, life and mostly, how to work with people with big personalities. Thank you for that window of memories.

I would also like to thank my family for their love and support. Among blood and genetics, it gives me pride that we all share such a love for food. It's part of who we are — we are lovers of life and tradition. There are also a handful of people I also feel that I need to thank, although it's a bit ridiculous as they are strangers: Van Morrison, Arctic Monkeys, Mayer Hawthorne, David Bowie and Sam Cooke (the only other Cooke in my kitchen!). I made most of these recipes while listening to their music. (I also perfected dancing while mixing).

Last but not least, I would like to thank the amazing team at Ryland Peters & Small. Thank you Cindy Richards, David Peters, and Julia Charles for giving me these opportunities. A huge, huge thank you also goes to Leslie Harrington, Peter Cassidy, Lizzie Harris, Emily Kydd, Tony Hutchinson and Iona Hoyle. These are the people who really made this book work. Their vision with what to do with the food, how the book should look and their ability to make these recipes the best they can be is so very much appreciated. I would also like to thank my brilliant editor, Nathan Joyce. His attention to detail, his eye for what works and his ability to see the finished product and skillfully set his vision in motion is an unbelievable gift. It takes a true person of strength to be an editor, especially mine. Finally, I would like to thank my former editor, Ellen Parnavelas, who helped bring this idea to life.